Leadership Strategies
for Ministers

Leadership Strategies for Ministers

Charles Somervill

H. Wayland Cummings

Editor and Technical Consultant

The Westminster Press
Philadelphia

Book design by Gene Harris

First edition

Published by The Westminster Press®
Philadelphia, Pennsylvania

PRINTED IN THE UNITED STATES OF AMERICA

9 8 7 6 5 4 3 2 1

Library of Congress Cataloging-in-Publication Data

Somervill, Charles.
  Leadership strategies for ministers.

  1. Clergy—Office. 2. Pastoral theology.
3. Christian leadership. I. Cummings, H. Wayland.
II. Title.
BV660.2.S628 1987   253   86-26788
ISBN 0-664-24062-3 (pbk.)

To Mollie

Contents

Introduction

Leadership is an act of communication undertaken in order to motivate members of an organization to do what the leader wants them to do. Leadership is validated when this communication is effective. It is not something that one possesses merely because of one's title or rank. Therefore, the minister or other church leader must face the question posed by a potential follower: "Why should I do what the church wants me to do?"

"Perhaps," says the follower, already formulating the answer, "I would do it because I see in the leader something that I like, or I find that the reasoning of the leader agrees with my own, or I gain from the leader what I want and avoid what I do not want." Assuming a common com mitment to Christ, the strategies and tactics encouraging these alternative responses set the stage for effective leadership in the church.

In an earlier book, *Overcoming Communication Barriers in the Church,* we presented the basic principles of communication and the scientific research upon which they are based. Since that time, another book, *Managing Communication in Organizations,* by H. Wayland Cummings, Larry W. Long, and Michael L. Lewis, has synthesized the growing body of research on organizational communication. The present book illustrates these research principles as they affect leadership in the church.

Henry P. Whittimore is the fictitious minister featured in

our narrative. As a leader, Henry is sometimes right, sometimes wrong, and often uncertain. He has learned that quick, decisive answers are more believable than halting, unsure ones. But quick answers, when used as a cover-up for uncertainty, eventually wear thin. Clarity without an underlying competence is meaningless. A leader must not only be a good on-the-spot communicator but must have a knowledge of organizations, groups, and the dynamics of personal relationships. The gift of gab by itself is not enough to separate the leader from the con artist.

Throughout his ministry, Henry is confronted by church members who give him advice. They, too, are sometimes right, sometimes wrong, but rarely ever do they seem uncertain of their advice. Business people, educators, hospital administrators, engineers, and lawyers (to name but a few) all know techniques that work in their own areas of expertise, so why not at church? Of course, these people will disagree among themselves as to how leadership works. And since professionally they move in separate worlds, they can take or leave each other's advice when it pertains to business leadership.

But when the issue of church leadership comes up, watch out! Everyone is part of this environment. There is a feeling of joint ownership with the minister. Some older members who have seen ministers come and go would not even concede this much involvement to the minister. They may see the minister as an itinerant employee! The feeling of "my church," coupled with an individual conception of "God's will," is unique to members of this organization. (In fact, if that feeling were lost, the church would suffer decline.) Add—to the overall purpose of seeking God's will —the belief that God is loving and forgiving, and a strong expectation is developed among the members of the congregation that the church is in the business of making people feel better. Above all else, church members expect to feel included in the family of God.

Henry P. Whittimore has his work cut out for him. He must be a leader and yet know how to include others in leadership roles, for church people must feel a sense of inclusion in decision making. The principle of inclusion puts the burden on ministers at least to listen to advice, even poor advice, and treat it with respect. But leaders must also listen to the self and discover what forces in their own personality help or hinder the act of leadership.

The definition of leadership as an act of communication hardly provides a clue to what the successful church leader must do to fulfill that function. Because of fundamental differences in the nature of organizations, what works in one area often will not work in another. The church must be considered for itself in order to find specific directions.

If you feel the same inadequacies that Henry faces in this book, welcome to the club. Leadership, especially church leadership, is too complex a process for perfectionists. As with the apostle Paul's battle with sin, we may still find ourselves in the "wrong" all too often. However, there is considerable profit in increasing our knowledge of when we are wrong and when we are right. The ability to be lovingly critical of one's own mistakes is an essential part of growth and maturity. If we know what we did wrong the first time (or more likely the second or third), then we can step back and laugh with Henry.

ONE

Eastwood Church

1

Henry as Minister of Eastwood Church

Henry P. Whittimore began his ministry in the little congregation of Eastwood Church. At one time, the church had many more members than the two hundred now on the rolls. But the town suffered the loss of two major industries, with a resulting decrease in population and tax revenues, and was left with only a few small industries, a struggling but persistent oil company, and a large private college. The college, a source of pride to the community, continued to show vitality, with steady growth and excellent academic credentials.

Half the church's membership reflected the influence of college faculty and administration. Older members referred to these people as the "new guard." One of Henry's strongest church officers was the academic dean, Jim Monroe, a relatively young man who also was credited with much of the college's continued success. Dean Monroe was formerly a professor of social psychology with a research background in organizational behavior. Henry discovered that Jim not only was a good friend but was an excellent adviser for getting things done in the church.

Henry possessed an insatiable curiosity and was willing and eager to learn from a variety of sources—from the continuing education seminars of his seminary, from lay people in his congregation, and from his own mistakes. Whatever his failings, he was not a know-it-all. People liked this quality in Henry; they knew they could talk to him without fear of condescension.

By his second year at Eastwood Church, Henry had become accustomed to going out after a board meeting for a cup of coffee with some of his officers. Henry thoroughly enjoyed these moments. After a serious meeting, it seemed to him, in the relaxed setting of the restaurant, that the officers were genuinely open and honest with each other. The conversations around the table reminded him of the late-night get-togethers he enjoyed in college. And so when another board meeting ended, Henry was eager to explore how their newest officer, George Franklin, really felt about his role in the church.

George was a bright executive in the local oil company, with very little experience in churches. Three years ago he had started attending services because of his wife's insistence. In a short time, he not only had become a believer but was one of the best teachers in the church school.

Leadership as defined by the nature of the organization

Henry had noticed George frowning when some decisions were made on the church budget. Jim Monroe had obviously noticed this too, because after the group had ordered coffee, Jim brought the subject up again.

"Tell me, George," Jim said, "were you suffering from indigestion when we discussed the church budget? There was such a pained look on your face."

"I guess I was expecting more intelligence than was evident at that meeting," George replied.

"Where do you think we went wrong?" another officer asked.

"For one thing," George answered, "when Jennifer Smith was presenting the funding needs of the little community group she works with outside the church, it seemed to me we voted yes because Jennifer wanted it— not because it was the best use of our mission money."

"Oh, well—" Henry fumbled for a reply. "I don't know

much about Jennifer's group, but I do know that Jennifer Smith has meant a lot to this church in her own financial giving. If I had been voting, it would be hard for me to go against a project that means so much to her."

"That sort of thing would never happen in the company I work for," George said, "and I certainly expect more of my church than of my company."

"You're saying that your company relates things more to the job than to people's feelings?"

"Yeah, well, shouldn't we be more concerned about mission than some individual's emotional involvement?"

"Henry, do you want to answer that?" Jim motioned to the waiter for more water.

Henry laughed. "Let's let someone else talk for a change."

"I'm not going to leave this table without an answer." George looked at Henry.

"Now, just a minute here," Jim said. "Let me take a crack at that question."

Henry breathed a sigh of relief.

Jim smiled. "Normally I'm paid very well for what I'm about to tell you," he went on. "You're getting it for free."

The others listened intently. Dean Monroe was widely respected in the community for his business seminars.

"Are you going to begin with purpose and objectives?" George asked.

"Not exactly," Jim said. "Let's start with an assumption often made in the literature that the best way to characterize an organization is by the primary product or output."

"OK." George grinned. "I'll tell you what the oil company primarily produces and then you tell me what the church primarily produces. My company produces a physical object called petroleum. Now describe the primary output of Eastwood Church."

Types of organizations

The others at the table laughed as they thought about the complexity of such a question.

"Not so fast," Jim objected. "Please complete your

analysis by telling us who produces your product, how it's produced, and how it's measured."

"Glad to oblige," George said amiably. "Our petroleum is produced by specialists through chemical and engineering technologies. The unit of measurement is volume. Any other questions?"

"Give us an idea of how your organization is designed and how problems are handled."

"We do it the old-fashioned way," George said, "with messages coming down from upper-level management. We have a specialist who deals with morale and job satisfaction, but basically we're out to get the job done, with upper management defining the problems and choosing solutions. Conflicts, the influencing of people, and so forth typically are managed by the upper level through rewards and punishments. Things get done efficiently and productively, and all the employees know where they stand."

"I see nothing wrong with that," Jim told him. "Of course, your company may see some changes in the next few years when the effectiveness of newer forms of management have been tested. But the carrot-and-stick approach you describe is still being used in many companies where the emphasis is on a concrete measure of productivity."

"No more stalling, Dr. Monroe," George said. "It's your turn to dazzle us with an organizational assessment of Eastwood. Tell me—just what is it that our church primarily produces?"

"Hmm." Jim laughed. "I may get into trouble on this one. First of all I should point out that a product is *output,* it's not necessarily a thing. It can be an intangible quality produced in humans. For example, a school can be said to produce educated people."

"What about churches?" someone asked impatiently.

"I don't know enough to answer for all churches," Jim said. "But in many churches such as ours, I would say that the primary product is a special type of person who finds need fulfillment through the church."

The nature of church organization

"What about *spiritual* need fulfillment?" asked George.

Henry joined in. "Which needs are spiritual and which ones aren't?"

"That would be a problem," agreed an older officer. "All sorts of needs can come up in the life of a congregation."

"I see that," George said. "Family counseling, deaths, financial problems, struggles of faith, and various other needs would involve every member in our church."

"In fact," Jim replied, "you might say that the church is in the business of making people feel good."

"Well-l-l." Henry paused for a moment. "I wouldn't say that's the *only* purpose. We have a mission which calls us outside the church and sometimes requires sacrifice. I'm not sure people always feel good about that mission, but it's at the heart of our purpose. And even if we say that the purpose is spiritual growth, aren't there some growing pains there?"

Jim nodded. "I see your point, but let me back up and put it another way. When it comes to the mission of the church, there may be some principles that aren't conducive to a sense of personal comfort. But I'm not really talking about that. I'm talking about the sense of individual worth that comes from our basic religious belief of trusting in a loving, forgiving God and becoming loving, forgiving persons ourselves. It gives us a sense of well-being. I'm not a theologian, and I suspect that the phrase 'making people feel good' would have to be carefully defined within theological limits. But if the church doesn't provide some way of showing how our lives are improved in the faith, people will stop going to church."

"No argument there," Henry said.

George laughed. "You wouldn't find this type of conversation in my oil company."

"No, you wouldn't. And that comment is right to the point," Jim said. "The difference in organizations can be seen in how we communicate. The church has a two-way personal emphasis about needs and goals. Problems and solutions are identified through shared personal experiences. Interdependence is assumed. Conflicts are resolved through appeals to the needs and emotional natures of people. And the only way that behavior can be influenced is by responding to these personal needs and goals in a way that's compatible with the purpose of the church. Therefore, need fulfillment is defined within the guidelines of the church, and our special type of person is produced accordingly. As you might guess, once the product of the organization has been described, the role of leader becomes an answer to production needs. But when we ask for an observable measurement of productivity in the church, we find an intangible product that defies measurement."

"So church leadership exists to meet the personal needs of people within the guidelines of the church," Henry said. He smiled. "Maybe that's why the Levite, in the story of the good Samaritan, passed by on the other side; the need didn't fit within his guidelines."

"Is the church unique as an organization?" asked another officer.

"I think it's unique," replied Jim. "I might get some argument from my colleagues. Some would say that the difference is just one of degree on a continuum of voluntary organizations. But I know of no other long-standing organization whose survival is so clearly dependent on the satisfaction of membership needs and goals. And where else do you get such debates as we have in the church—nearly always with someone getting up and making an appeal to our emotional natures? We're concerned not just with rational and work-related solutions but with who gets hurt and how people feel about it."

"We want everybody to win," Henry said.

"Precisely," Jim agreed. "We feel terrible if we can't find a win-win solution. But such a solution may not be possible because it requires a higher level of trust and openness than is present."

"And because of that, we sometimes feel hurt and have a lot of guilt," Henry observed.

"And people get angry and look for ways to get back!" said the oldest officer at the table.

"Good grief!" George exclaimed. "No wonder the officers backed off when Jennifer Smith presented an emotional appeal for funding her community project."

"We don't want to tread on people's feelings," Henry said.

George frowned. "I thought the church was a peaceful community where we learned to share honestly with one another."

"That's our purpose," Henry replied, "and in many ways we *are* a peaceful, loving community. But because of the dynamics that Jim described, it isn't always easy. As they say, 'Nothing worthwhile is easy.'"

"You can find more anger in churches than any other place on earth." Jim shook his head.

"And, one hopes, more love," Henry replied.

"I know one thing," George added, "I don't want to be a minister. I don't care how much they might pay me."

"Ministers have it rough," agreed another officer.

George leaned back in his chair and thought for a moment. "All right—now, Dr. Monroe, you've shed some light on the church as an organization," he said. "What advice do you have for our leader, the Reverend Henry P. Whittimore, in this powder keg you've described? How can he survive the contradictions inherent in the church as an organization both potentially loving and explosive?"

"Wait a minute," Henry objected, "I'm not the only leader in this church. All of you sitting here are leaders too. Our church believes in shared—"

"C'mon, Henry," Jim interrupted, "get off your high horse. Of course leadership is shared in the church; interdependence is assumed. But you know very well what George is getting at. Your role as a leader is not the same as our roles. You are ordained as a full-time minister, and that carries with it a whole bundle of expectations you can't escape by invoking the doctrine of the priesthood of all believers. You're a 'priest' of a different sort; you were hired to head the organization. This is not to say that you are any less human than the rest of us or that you should make all the decisions. But you have a *role*, Henry, a role as the minister of Eastwood Church, that people expect you to play. How well you are perceived as doing that determines your credibility."

"I'm frankly disappointed," Henry said. "I was hoping that you regarded me as a colleague."

"We respect you more than that," Jim responded. "Relax, Henry, you're among friends, and this discussion might do you some good. Sitting across from you is church officer Mitch Elwood, who happens to be a clinical psychologist. Mitch hasn't said one word in this discussion, but I know he has given seminars for church leaders. I want to hear what his thinking is on the leadership role of the minister."

Mitch smiled. "First of all, I don't know everything there is to know about the subject. But I do know that most ministers, psychologically, are in a double bind. You are in this loving, caring community called the church, which

Psychological implications for the leader

sometimes responds with emotions blown out of all proportion. An irrational attack on the minister from one member or another is always a possibility. In this environment, most ministers acquire a strong need to be liked and may feel crushed by an unkind word. And logically, if you are preaching love to others, you would expect to be loved in return."

"What's wrong with wanting to be loved—or at least liked?" asked Henry.

"The problem is not with just wanting to be liked," Mitch replied. "It's what you do when you aren't liked—especially if you have a strong need to be liked. For example, if I don't like you, and you don't care whether I like you or not, you have no problem, at least not psychologically.

But if you desperately want me to like you and I don't, what are you going to do about it?"

"I'm going to do everything I can to convince you that I am likable." Henry smiled as he spoke.

"And as a minister, probably you won't give up," Mitch continued. "A strong persistent need to be liked can lead to serious problems. You've seen movies where someone becomes obsessed with the need to be liked by another person. Such an obsession leads to an unhealthy preoccupation that overrides anything productive. Ministers with specific expectations of what the church should be can get into a real double bind when someone does not respond positively."

"What can we do?" Henry was intrigued.

"If you insist on everyone liking you, there's nothing that can be done for you. You're a hopeless case."

"So I have to face the awful fact that not everyone is going to like me," Henry said. "What happens to ministers who refuse to believe that?"

"Often they become passive-aggressive, choking down their anger and becoming more depressed than ever. Or they may rationalize that they are too superior for other people ever to realize their great worth. So they become arrogant and contemptuous of anyone who does not like them."

"I admit that I have a need to be liked," Henry said, "and maybe that's why I don't like giving up until I have tried

Ways of influencing people	every reasonable way to have an influence on someone else. But neither do I want to develop a compulsion. What's reasonable in trying to reach another person?"

"OK, let's say you want me to do you a favor. What are some ways you would try to get me to do that?"

"I don't know," Henry said. "Let me think."

"Come on, Henry," Mitch coaxed. "Tell me why I should do you a favor."

Henry laughed. "Because you like me."

"Don't laugh. That's a correct answer. If I like you, then I have a reason to do you a favor. Can you give me another reason?"

"Well, what if it makes good sense to you? Maybe you would be willing to do it if you believed it was for a good cause."

"Sure, if it makes sense to *me,* then I'll do you a favor. What's another reason?"

"That's all I can think of," Henry replied.

"How about a reward-punishment approach? You might convince me to do you a favor because of some personal benefit I might derive from doing it. OK? Now, how many ways can you influence me?"

"Three," Henry answered.

"So you don't have to approach everyone based on an assumption that they like you. You can use an 'it-makes-sense' approach—what social scientists call an *internalization strategy.* Or you can use a *compliance strategy,* based on some concrete reward or punishment. You have more power than you might think. If a leader feels that he or she has no influence or power, that leader becomes ineffective."

"But Henry doesn't have an equal choice among these strategies," Jim pointed out, "because an organization based on personal need fulfillment leans heavily on liking relationships—on what we call an *identification strategy.*"

"That's true," Mitch said. "However, we should emphasize that a good leader is a versatile manager and never rules out any approach or strategy that might fit a particular situation. I can think of a building-fund campaign we had several years ago where a compliance strategy worked very well."

"I know the one you're referring to," rejoined Jim, "and it did work in the sense that we raised the money. But there were a lot of hard feelings because church people don't like to give under pressure. It was a system where almost every leader in the church had to monitor someone else's giving. A compliance strategy requires that type of surveillance. And although I wouldn't rule it out, I would use it very carefully in churches."

"How would you define the power that a leader has in the identification approach?" asked one officer.

"It's an influence based on the leader's attractiveness," Mitch replied. "There has to be some importance or salience attached to a relationship for it to work."

"What causes one person to like another?" Henry asked.

"According to research on liking relationships, or 'affiliative behavior,' people like one another because (one) they are in close proximity and regularly interact, (two) they tend to reduce one another's stress or anxiety, (three) they help one another to avoid loneliness and insecurity, (four) they have similar personalities, values, and attitudes, and (five) they give one another a sense of community and comfort through cooperation with others."

"So if I fit some of those criteria, people will like me," Henry said.

"Probably, if they perceive those characteristics in you," Mitch answered. "Certainly, trust among church people is based on those things, and to be of any influence you have to have that trust."

"What you are saying is that most people in the congregation *do* have to like me," Henry responded. "How does that fit in with your caution on the need to be liked?"

"Well, it's true that the minister as an effective leader must be fairly well liked by most people, most of the time," Mitch replied. "However, you don't have to be worshiped and adored, or even loved as a close personal friend. You would want the congregation to love God that way, but your leadership is not jeopardized if they like you somewhat less."

Henry smiled. "Yes. I think I know what you mean. I can remember certain seminary professors that I liked—but I wouldn't want to live next door to them. I gues it's all right for our members to feel the same way about me."

"But the identification strategy is inefficient," George objected. "It's like a marriage. It requires constant attention to interpersonal relationships. You could never run an oil company with it."

"That's true," Jim agreed. "The supervisor would have to be constantly available and devoted to subordinates. And it's hard to measure productivity by the liking-relationship approach. You can see the difficulty we have in evaluating church staff."

"I can also see the difference between churches and oil companies," George concluded.

"What about internalization, or the it-makes-sense approach?" Henry asked. "What types of organizations depend on that one?"

"Educators in a school system or doctors in a hospital should find that approach useful," Jim answered. "Internalization comes from inside the belief system of the individual. It's content-oriented, with decisions derived from the rational content of agreed-upon values. It also requires a situation where you have time to weigh decisions and outcomes within a high-trust environment. When decisions have to be made on the spot, you don't have time to use the it-makes-sense approach. But when you need participation and cooperation among colleagues, internalization usually is the best strategy—given the time to work through it."

"I think we use that strategy among church officers," Henry said. "We take our time, listen to committee reports, and try to come up with rational outcomes—at least we do sometimes."

"Sure, which goes back to Mitch's comment that more than one strategy is needed in any organization," Jim pointed out.

"And I would agree with Jim's comment that basically the church must be sensitive to the maintenance of healthy interpersonal relationships," Mitch said.

"I'm interested in maintaining good relationships," Henry said. "But I'm also concerned about effecting changes in people, of increasing their awareness and sensitivity to the needs of others."

"Identification is a very good strategy for effecting changes," Jim said. "All you have to do is look at the norms that control people's behavior and start from there. If we pride ourselves on being a generous, forgiving, other-oriented community, you can appeal to those qualities in developing people in the church. I think our members will identify with you if you show that you value those characteristics in your treatment of them. But don't start by assuming we have a theological sophistication akin to your own. Very few of us could identify with that. Your credibility is based on how compassionate we think you are, not how smart. Also, there may be some moral sanctions peculiar to our community that you need to be aware of."

"So much for my seminary training," Henry quipped. "At least *you* get to use your graduate work."

"Oh, no, use your theological training," Mitch replied. "But do it gradually and don't overload us. What Jim means is that most of us will be looking at who you are rather than listening to what you say."

"And don't try to fool us, Henry," Jim continued. "We know you are not all that different from the rest of us. We just want to see that you try a little harder than we do and that when you do goof you admit it. That way we won't feel so bad about your trying to influence our behavior."

"I'm beginning to get the picture," Henry said. "I guess I have to live with these role expectations. Maybe it's not so bad if it helps people see me as a credible source. At least that way they'll listen to me."

CONCLUSION

It is hard for people in fields other than the ministry to understand the nature of church administration. Certainly there is room for improvement, but at least one of the reasons for the apparent inefficiency of the church is inherent in the nature of its organization. When an organization sets out over the centuries to meet spiritual and personal needs without an observable product to sell or a bill of goods to present to clients, its influence or "power" will be related to the need fulfillment of its members.

Unless a cultlike position is taken, requiring absolute compliance from constituents, this fulfillment is likely to rely on identification behavior, with the minister leading the way as a model friend. Internalization, the it-makes-sense strategy, also may play a part if the church offers a rationalized, systematic approach. But every minister is under the constraint of practicing what he or she preaches. In the American church, this way often is one of comfort, friendship, and forgiveness. If the minister is perceived as a compassionate person, the leadership of the minister gains credibility. If not, then, regardless of other competencies, the minister will be less effective as a leader.

Add to the foregoing dynamics the doctrine of a loving, forgiving God, and the uniqueness of the church emerges more clearly. Seminars on rationally structured efficiency techniques may be helpful, but they usually have limited application to the church. Probably the best approach for a minister is to develop skills appropriate to the nature of church organization—leading the way as a friend, learning why people like people, and discovering techniques that build cohesion and a sense of community.

Even so, it is true that no leader should be ignorant of alternative approaches to influencing behavior. If the roof is falling in, or warring factions appear in the congregation, or social justice demands a speedy answer, then an identification strategy may not be adequate.

Whatever strategy is selected, no wise leader prepares for battle without a knowledge of what is required. Compliance will not work without continual monitoring of behavior in a system of observable rewards and punishments. Internalization will not work without a high level of trust and respect for fellow workers and for the job to be done. Identification will not work without a leader who is liked and represents the best ideals of the organization. If only a few of these conditions are present, the leader would do well to put the situation on hold. There is no disgrace in buying time to wait for a clearer solution to emerge.

Henry P. Whittimore has learned the principles for influencing behavior, or what social scientists call "behavior regulation." But applying these principles, as Henry will learn in the years ahead, requires a careful consideration of the people involved and the type of situation.

2

An Identification Strategy

Henry thought often of the home church in which he was reared and of the way in which his minister, Dr. Tom Anderson, approached members of the congregation. Dr. Anderson deplored such terms as behavior regulation, strategies, and tactics. In Dr. Anderson's day, most ministers felt uncomfortable with any such terms from the field of management. Yet it was obvious that Dr. Anderson intuitively understood how to approach people on the basis of liking relationships. He made a point of getting to know the needs of individuals, making himself available for drop-in chats, helping members in times of emotional stress and anxiety, and giving lonely individuals a sense of friendship and community. Dr. Anderson did not consider these things as tactics for behavior regulation. He was motivated by a sincere desire to help people. But Dr. Anderson usually got what he wanted in the programs of the church. The reason that he succeeded was crystal clear—the members loved him with all their hearts and souls and responded to practically everything he asked.

Henry was just as eager to help people as Dr. Anderson. But Henry knew that his own personality probably was perceived as more analytical and less patient than his home minister's. Henry was liked and respected but not warmly and enthusiastically loved. He remembered Mitch Elwood's warning about trying too hard to be liked and contented himself with fulfilling the image of a young minister doing a good job. He felt pride, and at times a little envy, in the way his wife, Janet, was received by the congregation. Janet was like that disciple in the Bible who was "loved most." Henry would have enjoyed that type of attention.

After coming home from her work in school administration, Janet spent much of her time hearing the emotional problems of members. But when members wanted to discuss a task-related problem, they came to Henry. Henry learned to confer with Janet and others like her before making committee appointments in order to select people who would work well together. The ability of a member to perform a task was never enough; the ability to relate to others had to be considered as well. When Henry thought of the patience and the enormous amount of time required to hear personal problems, he was less envious of and more grateful for Janet's abilities.

This type of respect and sharing presented an ideal situation within Eastwood Church. It flourished for several years until Henry was faced with a crisis so traumatic that everything he had accomplished seemed meaningless. That awful day came when Harold Robbins, the most venerable member of Eastwood Church, walked slowly into Henry's office and sat down in dead silence.

"It's good to see you, Mr. Robbins," Henry said uneasily.

"I wish I could say the same," Harold replied.

"Is there something wrong?" Henry could feel the palms of his hands beginning to sweat.

"I wish I could think of an easier way to say this. It hurts me deeply, Henry, but I feel that I must tell you something," Harold began. "I have been observing your attempt to be our minister for some time now. You lack the compassion we need in the minister of this church. You ought to consider going into some other profession—a job where you won't be involved with people. If it wasn't for your wife, Janet, you wouldn't have lasted this long."

"What do you mean?" Henry hoped that he was having a bad dream.

"You've treated this church with the sensitivity of that new computer you put in the secretary's office. Don't ask me to give you a specific example. I don't know that I could give you one. It's in your voice, the way you behave toward your members. How is it that you've never called me by my first name? Why is it always 'Mr. Robbins' this and 'Mr. Robbins' that?"

"I call you Mr. Robbins out of respect," Henry said.

"I expect *children* to call me 'Mr. Robbins,' not my minister," Harold said. "There's a plastic quality about you, Henry. Even your sermons are like words coming off an assembly line, put together as your seminary manufactured them—no feeling, only words. When you stand at the door after the worship service, you still get the names of people confused. You just don't care, Henry; you really don't care."

"I do care!"

"I'm sorry, Henry. I've talked to other officers, and no one really believes that about you. The members will no longer respond to you. It never was your church. You just aren't effective here. I would advise you to make your plans to move on—before it's too late."

"Please—" Henry was speechless. "I don't know what to say."

"There's nothing more to say," Harold replied. "In my business, when I had to let an employee go, I gave him two weeks. I don't see why your case should be different. But in any event, I don't see this thing dragging out over a long time. Otherwise, we'll have to make a formal request. You don't want that. Now—I've said all that I'm going to say."

And Harold Robbins left the office as quietly as he had come, leaving Henry in a state of shock.

For the next two weeks, Henry mentioned this episode to no one. He found it increasingly difficult to concentrate on anything except routine matters. His sermons seemed impossible to prepare, and he felt as if a black hole were swallowing him up. Finally, he made an appointment to see Mitch Elwood.

"You got burned and you're feeling a little paranoid," Mitch said, after hearing Henry's story. "Now, what do you want to do?"

"Resign, I guess," Henry replied.

"Do you really want to do that?" Mitch asked.

"No, but what are my alternatives?" Henry stared blankly out the window.

"Well"—Mitch tossed his pencil onto his desk—"so far there hasn't been much said except to you. I doubt if Harold has mentioned this to anyone else. He wanted you to *think* he had, but probably he hasn't. I haven't heard anything."

"But he's going to say something sometime." Henry frowned.

"He might if people start commenting on how depressed you're acting," Mitch responded. "He'll need to hear something bad about you from others so that he can build on it. I know Harold. He won't start anything in public without some prompting. Harold will avoid looking like a troublemaker."

Henry suddenly realized that he knew very little about Harold Robbins, outside the fact that members referred to him as "Mr. Eastwood." Harold was largely responsible for the founding of Eastwood Church.

"You're saying that I have some time before Harold builds enough support to get me out." Henry gave a weak smile. "That's very reassuring."

"I really don't think he'll be successful, Henry," Mitch said, "unless you become super-defensive about every criticism that people make of you. You just need to hold your own and continue to do a good job here at Eastwood. Let Harold Robbins take care of himself."

Henry took Mitch's advice and tried to put the incident out of his mind. Everything seemed to go along smoothly until two months later, when Harold complained at the board meeting that Henry had not come to visit him in the hospital. Furthermore, Harold mentioned one other member who was sick and whom Henry had failed to visit.

Henry apologized and said that he was unaware of Harold's stay in the hospital. As it turned out, Harold was being treated for a suspected stroke and was in and out of the hospital within a twenty-four-hour period. Henry could find no one who knew that Harold had been there. The other person whom Harold reported as overlooked was an inactive member who was suffering from the flu. Henry suspected that Harold was trying to paint a picture of a non-caring person—a minister's most vulnerable point. Henry decided to talk to Jim Monroe and explore some ways to improve relations with Harold.

"I don't know," Jim said. "You've got a big problem. I may lose my guru license on this one, but I'll give it a try. Let's start out by looking at Harold Robbins. What does he value most?"

"That's easy," Henry replied. "He's 'Mr. Eastwood' and he values that reputation."

"Right. Harold remembers the church when it was at its zenith. He's always talking about how he hopes to see the church come back as strong as it was. For a while, he agreed with many of our members who believe that economic and population losses make that expectation unrealistic. But Harold has suffered some minor strokes, and it may be that he is returning to the past and desperately trying to regain what was. Probably he wants to see a return to old-time evangelism, with little or no emphasis on social issues. It also might be that he sees Henry P. Whittimore as—"

Dealing with alienation

"—as the reason why Eastwood Church has failed to grow." Henry finished Jim's sentence. "Get rid of me, and everything will be all right again."

"Exactly," Jim said. "I hope you don't think less of yourself, even though it's hard not to take Harold's attack personally. Most likely, any minister serving at Eastwood would have the same problem. You just happened to be here at the wrong time for the church to grow."

"All of which means that Harold is going to keep coming after me." Henry sighed.

"Of course he is." Jim nodded. "But you did the right thing by doing nothing at all these past two months. Too many leaders react to a possible threat before letting some time go by to see what actually happens. Often, the leader gives way to the emotional upheaval of the moment and makes things worse. You lost nothing by keeping your cool and discovering the extent of Harold's ego involvement on the issue."

"Well, now that I've discovered it, what's next?" Henry asked.

"Use that analytical mind of yours and look at the facts," Jim said. "One thing in your favor is that Harold has not made a public comment about your dismissal. What someone says in private does not carry the same emotional commitment as it does in public."

"That's why our church believes in public professions of faith."

"True," Jim said quietly. "But you also know that Harold is carrying a heavy anchor on what should be done about his church. He has set that anchor down where there are very few acceptable alternatives to your leaving. Certainly he is not going to listen to any argument from you. Can you think of anyone with a high regard for you to whom he might listen?"

"Jennifer Smith fits that description," Henry answered with a glimmer of hope. "Harold thinks the world of Jennifer!"

"Good choice," Jim continued. "Now think hard. What could Jennifer say to Harold that might make a difference?"

"That I'm a good guy?"

Jim laughed. "No, that contrasts to what Harold already believes about you. Think of a continuum with nine statements expressing the various degrees of how someone is liked. What the congregation believes about Henry P. Whittimore can be expressed from 'not liking you at all, liking you very little, liking you somewhat'—all the way to 'liking you very much.' Probably Harold would reject any statement on the continuum beyond 'liking you very little.' "

"Good grief!" Henry exclaimed. "There's nothing that Jennifer can say. Harold is not going to listen to anything good about me."

"Well, certainly you can rule out any arguments on your inherent good qualities," Jim said. "But does that exhaust all the possible arguments that might change Harold's position just a little?"

"What good does it do to change Harold's position just a little?" Henry asked. "He's still going to want to throw me out."

"Think of the ocean slowly pulling the sand away from the shore," Jim said. "It can't be done all at once, but the ocean keeps coming back for more and more until the shoreline itself is changed. And the people walking on the beach are probably not aware that these changes are taking place."

"I'll have to remember that one for a sermon illustration," Henry quipped. "Seriously, I don't think I have time for these little changes to take place."

"Yes, you do—as long as Harold doesn't go public with his feelings about you," Jim replied.

"Isn't there some technique or method that will work faster in changing Harold's mind?" Henry asked.

"Not in a sensitive situation with a strong ego involvement," Jim said. "Let's put this matter in perspective. First of all, you need to work with someone who likes you— Jennifer Smith—whom Harold also likes. That's the identification approach; it requires someone with whom Harold can identify. Then you choose an appropriate tactic."

"Fine. What do you call this 'shifting sands' tactic and what sort of appeal can you make?" Henry felt a sense of growing frustration.

"In research literature, it's derived from social judgment theory," Jim answered. "Each of us makes a judgment about a given issue. Some arguments that can be made about a judgment fall within the latitude of rejection, some are neutral, and some fall within the latitude of acceptance."

"And the more arguments that one rejects, the stronger the ego involvement with the issue," Henry said. "Harold is a good example. Probably he would reject all arguments except the ones based on 'not liking me at all' and 'liking me very little.' "

Tactical use of social judgment

"That's correct." Jim suspected that Henry had read some of the literature on the subject. "We can hope that Harold's present position, or anchor point, 'not liking you at all,' will find some way to move up the continuum. But you understand why Harold is carrying a heavy anchor. He has a high ego involvement with a very narrow latitude of acceptance."

"I can't imagine what would move him," Henry responded. "Obviously, Jennifer would have to make an argument that would fall within Harold's latitude of acceptance. How is that going to change his position?"

"You don't aim an argument at his anchor point," Jim said. "You aim just a little beyond that, within his latitude of acceptance but toward the neutral zone."

"We've already ruled out any appeal made on behalf of my good character. What's left?" Henry asked.

"Maybe an appeal for the good of the church." Jim pondered the idea for a moment. "What if you are seen as a necessary evil—strike that. Let's call it a matter of expediency. Jennifer Smith could argue that the church is still struggling to regain some of the old traditional ways of doing things. She could say that we may not like the way things are going now, but if we switched pastors at this point, the younger members might try to get in someone even less evangelistic than Henry P. Whittimore. At the moment we have a compromise in Whittimore, who at least responds to the financial power, if not the values, of the old guard. Get the picture?"

"Yeah, and I don't like it. I'm not that way. I believe in evangelism, even if it is difficult to make gains at Eastwood. I also believe in our denominational programs on social issues. I see both sides, and I don't see them as mutually exclusive. In fact, I think it's an old worn-out debate that most people have resolved. And I certainly don't see myself as catering to our wealthier members!"

"Henry, nobody sees you that way except Harold," Jim said. "But Harold is never going to get a chance to see any good in you unless we slowly move him away from his current anchor point. If he shifts his position on you to one of an expedient compromise, maybe we can convince him that you have some other redeeming values on the next go-round. . . . We can leave out the part about your favoring the wealthy."

"Thank you. I get the point," Henry replied, "and I'll talk to Jennifer. I hope Harold will stop seeing horns on me."

When Henry talked to Jennifer Smith, she expressed some reservations about Jim Monroe's strategy. One of the things that bothered her was the possible appearance of deception.

"I'm not trying to moralize on the subject," Jennifer began, "and I realize that one hundred percent honesty would do away with ninety percent of diplomacy and tact. But I don't want to come across as a phony. Harold Robbins knows me too well. I'm sure he's aware of the fact that I have a lot of respect for you. After all, I was on the search committee that brought you here. If I suddenly paint a picture of you as an expedient compromise, he's not going to buy it."

"Then what's left?" Henry asked.

"I don't know. Let me keep what Jim suggested in mind," Jennifer replied. "I'll take a reading on Harold, and if that anchor is as heavy as you think, I may take Jim's advice—in one form or other. Harold is like a second father to me, and I would have to say something that fits within that relationship."

Jennifer Smith waited a few days until Harold Robbins invited her out to lunch, something he did customarily. Jennifer did not want to jump into a defense of Henry and looked for an unobtrusive way to broach the subject. Fortunately, Harold brought it up first.

"I am very much disappointed with Henry Whittimore," Harold began. "I know that you were on his search committee, but I think you missed on that one."

"I can't be perfect all the time." Jennifer laughed. "But Henry really is in a tight spot. I feel sorry for him. He's got the old guard on one side and the new guard on the other."

"Bull!" Harold replied. "Whittimore has sold out to those liberals. I couldn't see it at first. But his sermons have shown him for what he is—all social issues and no evangelism. No wonder this church hasn't grown! Whittimore is a wolf in sheep's clothing, a snake in the grass!"

Jennifer was surprised at Harold's open vehemence. Certainly Jennifer would not be doing Henry any favors by making an impassioned rebuttal. Furthermore, Harold was behaving uncharacteristically; head-on encounters were not his style. The problem was that Harold carried a lot of support from the old guard. And if his friends saw the normally easygoing Harold ready to do battle, they easily might be spurred on to enlist against Henry. Harold's physical condition would not even be considered as a contributing cause of his combativeness. The tactic that Jim Monroe suggested seemed to be the only alternative.

"I can see that there is a serious situation developing here," Jennifer agreed. "But that situation could be made even worse by getting rid of Henry."

"I don't see that at all," Harold said.

"Look at Henry's background," Jennifer said. "He was raised in a conservative church by conservative parents. He was in one of our best seminaries—with excellent training in the Bible. Henry may have been swayed by some new influences, but a child never forgets those values taught at a young age. And Henry has had more than enough training in the right way. If we elected a new search committee, you know our new guard would insist on representation. You can imagine what would happen then."

"What?" asked Harold.

"Who would have the most time to do the traveling on that search committee?" Jennifer said rhetorically. "Not our older members; they have too many responsibilities here at home. Who would have the most connections outside the state? Those new-guard people have been all over the world. We could end up with such a liberal that Henry Whittimore would look like a fundamentalist!"

"That's a nightmare," said Harold. "I won't stand by and have my church destroyed!"

"You won't have to," Jennifer responded. "We still have enough good people on the board to point things in the right direction. Why don't you leave Henry Whittimore to me?"

"No, I think we both should work on him," Harold objected. "When I see Whittimore getting out of line, I'm going to let him know it. If Whittimore stays, he's going to hear from me."

Jennifer laughed again. "Well, perhaps between the two of us, we can keep Whittimore on the straight and narrow."

Later, when Jennifer Smith reported to Jim and Henry, they reviewed what had happened thus far. Jim was pleased with the outcome of Jennifer's visit with Harold Robbins.

"At least Harold won't push so hard to get Henry out," Jim said. "I think Jennifer moved his anchor point, and just maybe Harold will soften his attitude and become—uh, a loyal gadfly."

"Right now he sounds more like an angry hornet," Henry said.

"Or a bee in your bonnet." Jennifer laughed.

"I don't like bees in my bonnet," Henry shot back. "I'm allergic to beestings, and I don't want to worry about what Harold will do next."

"You don't have to worry about it," Jim said. "You know what Harold will do. He's going to take a potshot at you every time he gets a chance. But that's better than a systematic campaign to get you out. And we're not finished —I think eventually Harold can come to respect you."

"How's that going to happen?" Jennifer asked.

"Slowly, one step at a time," Jim replied. "Harold needs to hear good things about Henry from other people within Harold's inner circle."

Broadening liking relationships

"In other words, we have to market Henry P. Whittimore so that Harold's friends will become supporters," Jennifer said. "That may take some doing."

"Not exactly. Henry will want to know the needs of these people and how to minister to them," Jim reflected. "That shouldn't be too hard. Most of them would be delighted to receive a nice long visit from their minister. They represent our retired folks who sometimes are neglected by the church."

"I must admit I haven't visited these people as often as I should," Henry said. "I think I know most of the people you're referring to. But I would appreciate your making a list with some notations as to background."

"We can do that," Jennifer promised. "And you'll enjoy getting to know these members, Henry. They're charming people."

Henry felt some guilt for visiting members to save his own hide, but that feeling soon subsided after three months of steady calling. He found the visits were valuable in themselves. He learned something new, or rather he rediscovered an old principle. People in the church like to feel included as important members in the family of believers. And there was a special sense of community among the older members that derived from a history of pleasant memories in the church. Henry had forgotten how the church at one time was the center of social activities. He saw the possibility of restoring some of those values by providing a home Bible study within that group. Before long, he was meeting regularly with them and thoroughly enjoying it.

Six months passed, and Henry heard very little from Harold Robbins. The week before Christmas, Henry met as usual with his home Bible group. As he was sitting there, listening to their discussion, he realized how much he loved these older people; they supplied him with more genuine affection than any other group in the church. God bless you, Harold Robbins, Henry said to himself. Without you, I never would have discovered these people.

The phone rang. The caller was Mrs. Robbins, who asked Henry to come to the hospital. Harold had had a severe stroke. When Henry arrived, Harold was conscious but his voice was weak and his words came slowly.

"Henry"—Harold motioned him to come closer—"I want to tell you something."

"Don't try to talk, Harold," Henry said sympathetically.

"I need to tell you." Harold struggled to control his breathing. "I've been wanting to come to your Bible study. I—uh, I felt too ashamed."

"If it hadn't been for you there wouldn't be any Bible study," Henry confessed with a smile. "I did it just to prove to your friends that I was a good minister. I wanted you to hear about it and not hate me any more. I'll tell you one thing—I've come to love those people."

Harold laughed, then coughed. "Maybe we—we both learned something."

Harold recovered after surgery, and Henry was a frequent caller at his home. The Bible study grew, and Henry found that many of his better sermons were attributable to that group.

CONCLUSION

An identification strategy takes more imagination than one of internalization or compliance. The appeal is to the emotions through friendships. If there is a conflict, restoring the relationship by openly discussing the problem with the disgruntled party may not work. When there is a perceived violation of trust, which is often the case in interpersonal conflicts, an appeal to reason usually goes out the window. The best technique may be to enlist an intermediary who is friendly to both parties. The most persuasive argument is one that fits within a belief that the person already accepts on an emotional level. The argument has to sound like something that is for the person's own good. It cannot be based on the good of the offender.

Many conclusions about the ways that attitudes change are based on research done with groups of people. Therefore, when one selects a strategy from social science, such as social judgment, its application to a relationship between just two people must be flexible. For example, when Jim Monroe suggested what Jennifer Smith might say to Harold Robbins, the message that Jennifer delivered had to be modified to fit within her actual relationship with Harold. Since Jennifer looked up to Harold as a "second father," an approach could not be based on being colleagues of equal status. Jennifer needed to show Harold a special deference in keeping with their relationship. Otherwise, Harold would disregard the content of the message because the approach used to deliver it seemed inappropriate.

The general principle of the social-judgment technique has been thoroughly tested. It is a sound procedure for bringing about attitude change that is relatively permanent. An effective use of this tactic will first of all determine the extent of the person's ego involvement with an issue. Since Harold Robbins rejected more arguments than he accepted for retaining the services of Henry P. Whittimore, his ego involvement could be determined as high. With a strong ego involvement, any change will be extremely slow. In fact, if a person becomes aware of a deliberate attempt to change his or her attitude, this tactic certainly will fail. Harold had to be brought along slowly without being aware of the change. That procedure meant starting within the narrow confines of his latitude of acceptance and slowly expanding that latitude by moving just a little bit beyond his anchor position. He could not see any good at all in Whittimore, so the only argument that he would tolerate for retaining him would be for the good of the church. And even that argument had to make sense within Harold's values.

As to the actual change, "cognitive dissonance," a sense of betraying one's own values (a tactic described in the next chapter), played a part. In order to move Harold, the implied threat of ending up with someone worse than Whittimore had to be felt on an emotional level. Harold was made to feel that he might inadvertently destroy his church by opening the door for a more liberal minister if he got rid of Henry. And Harold responded, "I won't stand by and have my church destroyed!"

Happy endings, such as the one Henry experienced with Harold, unfortunately are not always available in such conflicts. But they do happen, even in churches. Henry found his way into the hearts of Harold's friends, and that's a potent remedy. However, if Harold had not undergone the slight change from his initial anchor point, there would have been no happy ending. Harold would have greeted the news of a "changed" Henry with incredulity. And once Harold had gone public with a campaign to get rid of Henry, the chances of an attitude change of any sort would have been practically none. The only alternative would have been all-out war with Harold. Henry most likely would have been dragged into a mud-slinging contest, with character assassination on both sides. And even if Henry had won such a battle, Harold would not have stayed a loser for long. Losers don't stay losers in churches. They try again. Eventually, the war would have taken its toll, with Henry suffering the consequences. The best choice in such a situation may indeed be the resignation of the minister.

The worst did not happen. Henry not only survived his ordeal but found some new friends. He regained a sense of confidence in his role as a minister and even transcended his analytical personality. He looked for ways of building personal relationships with his parishioners and could see no use whatsoever in a strategy of compliance. The identification and internalization approaches seemed to be the only ones needed at Eastwood Church. But when a leader rules out a strategy, that can be a mistake—as Henry will find out later on in his ministry.

TWO

First Church

3

Henry as an Associate at First Church

After seven years at Eastwood, Henry took a new position as an associate minister of First Church. He made that decision because he wanted to serve as apprentice to Dr. Arthur Wellborn, one of the most respected senior ministers in Henry's denomination. Not only was Dr. Wellborn an excellent preacher, he also had a good working knowledge of interpersonal relationships.

Both Henry and Janet had gone through some significant changes from their experience at Eastwood. Henry was more confident as a minister, having weathered the storms at Eastwood. But Janet wanted more distance between herself and the members of the congregation. She remembered the pain that Henry suffered, but she had not shared in the dialogues and decisions that led to a resolution of the conflict. As a result, Janet felt more of a sense of hurt than victory in Henry's winning the friendships of Harold Robbins and other members of Eastwood. She was still warm and understanding but more interested in pursuing her own career than participating in Henry's.

Fortunately, the members of First Church did not want the spouses of their staff to become overly involved in the work of the church. Some members recalled a period of hurt feelings, anger, and turmoil over just such an involvement. The dynamics were similar to the crisis that Henry and Janet faced at Eastwood. It was hard for Janet to recover from a strong threat delivered to her husband, especially when her identification with the Eastwood congregation had been so intimate.

Henry's responsibilities at First Church included working with the Church Growth Committee, the Community Service Committee, and the Hospital Care Committee and assisting Dr. Wellborn in the worship services. After the first year of Henry's stay at First Church, Dr. Wellborn expanded Henry's duties to include additional preaching opportunities and serving on ad hoc committees that dealt with policies and decision making. Henry was obtaining a better sense of how the organization of First Church worked as a whole.

In every church, there is a glue that holds it together. This glue is derived from a combination of norms, values, and rules—written and unwritten—and their resulting expectations—spoken and unspoken. To make matters more complicated, many of these expectations are somewhat different from those which ministers have learned in seminary. A long, intense program of education makes this difference inevitable. Perhaps this

An internalization strategy

is one reason why some seminaries provide a sophisticated program on organizational and communication behavior.

Henry Whittimore strongly believed, in keeping with his seminary training, that the church should be open to all people and that every person is of equal spiritual value in the sight of God. Furthermore, it seemed to Henry that the members of First Church felt the same way. After all, the church included members of different ethnic groups, and they worked well together in the programs of the church.

And so, when the community around First Church began to grow with new hi-tech industries, Henry was pleased to see that his visitation efforts as an associate were paying big dividends in the influx of many new members. In fact, First Church increased its membership by 20 percent over a four-year period. At first, the worship services were filled to capacity on most occasions. But then attendance began to decline, and some of the old, established members transferred their memberships. Fewer people were willing to accept such responsibilities as teaching in the church school, serving as a church officer, and singing in the choir. The staff became more critical of each other as nothing they tried seemed to correct the situation. They created new fellowship opportunities, changed the order of the worship service, and provided a new curriculum in the church school, and the choir even experimented with new types of music. But apparently none of these things worked.

By the fifth year of Henry's ministry at First Church, the officers decided to try to find the causes of the church's declining statistics. A committee was set up to study the matter, and Henry was asked to submit his own evaluation. After six months, the committee had reached no consensus and Henry was just as frustrated as before. Finally, Art Wellborn invited Henry into his office along with the other associate minister, Ruth Benson, and a church officer, Paul Holtman. Paul was a professor of communication. Henry had enjoyed talking with Paul and Art about many of the same concepts that he and Jim Monroe had discussed at Eastwood.

"We've worried about the changes at First Church many times," Art began, "and nothing we've done has made any difference. I want a solution. If it means my leaving First Church, I'll do it—whatever it takes. We started with a big increase in our programs, and now we're going downhill. What's the problem?"

"It's not you personally, Art," Paul responded. "The members are happy with you—and your staff is doing a good job too."

"How can that be true with our declining statistics?" Henry asked.

"Well, maybe it's just the times," Paul said. "Churches are not as popular as they used to be."

"But other churches in the city are not experiencing our

problems," Ruth objected. "No one had as big a boom as we did, followed by as big a bust!"

"And it isn't that our new members aren't involved in the life of the church," Henry commented. "They have key positions in every program of our church. So what is it? Do our old members not get along with the new?"

"I can't believe that," Art replied. "Our members have always prided themselves on their openness to others."

"Our established members really aren't that much older," Paul added. "The new members are only a few years younger than the rest of us."

"We sound just like the committee that was set up to study this matter," Art said. "In my opinion, we've come up empty. I know something's wrong, but I can't put my finger on it."

"Maybe we need a not-so-friendly investigator to come in and take a look at what's going on," Paul replied.

"What do you mean?" asked Ruth.

"When you love a church as we do," Paul answered, "you may be a little too close to the situation to make an objective assessment. We need someone who hasn't got anything at stake here to do an evaluation."

"Who?" asked Henry.

"A real hard-nosed troubleshooter," Paul said. "The person I'm thinking of has done a number of organizational communication studies, for both profit and nonprofit groups. Her name is Beth Lexington. She has a Ph.D. in Organizational Communication. She doesn't look as tough as she is—she has an easy way of interviewing people. But when she reports to the board, everything is put down in simple, direct language with no feelings spared. One voluntary organization she assessed was so upset by her report that the board members came close to resigning."

"Do you think we could handle something like that?" Henry wondered.

"It should be fun," Art replied. "I don't think our board members are all that fragile. We could use an honest assessment."

When the board discussed the matter of hiring Dr. Lexington, they agreed to give her complete cooperation and to keep her conclusions confidential. There was some apprehension, but no one had a better solution.

When Beth Lexington arrived, Henry was pleased to see a warm, outgoing person with charm and a sense of humor that would make most church members feel comfortable. Beth began her interview with Henry by asking for information about the number of new members who had joined the church and other related data to help her get a better picture of the congregation. Then she asked for his view of the situation.

An organizational communication assessment

"On our way over to your office, you said that your troubles began when you started taking in new members. How did you assimilate them into your church?"

"Oh, I don't think that we have a problem there," Henry said. "We have a great assimilation program. Our visitation committee makes at least two personal visits to their homes. We find out what things they would enjoy doing at the church, and then we have the chairpersons of respective committees contact them and get them involved. When the new members meet with our board, each of our programs is described so they get a feel for the total picture of our church organization. We then assign an officer to act as sponsor for each new member or family. The sponsors invite the new members over for an informal evening or dinner and help them get acquainted with other members of the congregation. We like to make our new members feel important, and we get them into positions of leadership as soon as possible."

"Sounds like a well-organized approach that a new member would like." Beth smiled. "How have your established members responded? Have you received any criticisms of the new members?"

"Nothing major." Henry thought for a moment.

"I want to hear about the minor things too," Beth said.

"Well, it's hardly worth mentioning, but Barbara Johnston, one of our church school teachers, did complain about the behavior of some of our new teenage members. Apparently, Barbara doesn't like them kissing in the church hallways. As far as I'm concerned, it's no big deal."

"These teenagers come from families associated with the new hi-tech industries in town, right? What about your established teenagers—where do their parents work?" Beth asked.

"We have doctors, lawyers, administrators, corporation executives, teachers, accountants, public health workers, and a variety of other people. The salary range is not that different from the hi-tech families."

"Where do the new teenagers go to school?" Beth asked.

"There's a new high school out in that area of town that takes in most of them. Probably that's why the hi-tech kids stick together."

"Hmm," Beth said. "Those facts may be important."

"If you can come up with a solution to our problems with just that information, more power to you!" Henry replied.

Beth laughed. "We need to define the problem first before we get to the solution. I'll talk to some more people and then do my report."

One month passed, and Beth Lexington was ready to make her report to the board. The officers had agreed that everyone would hear her at the same time. Beth wanted her ideas to have an open hearing without the prejudice of previous exposures. Even Art was not allowed a preview.

"First off," Beth began as she addressed the board, "I'm going to give you a diagnosis of the situation before we get into remedies and suggested solutions. I've conducted all my interviews, but the specific comments I received will be kept confidential.

"In general, the members of your congregation have a

strong identification with First Church and seem pleased with the staff and the board."

"We already knew that," one of the board members complained.

"Obviously, you feel that something is terribly wrong or you wouldn't have hired me," Beth continued. "What I find that may be wrong is the perception shared by leaders of this church about what is going on. And by leaders I mean the staff and the board members."

The members of the board became silent at this point and gave Beth their undivided attention.

"You decided, because you gained twenty percent in new members and then saw some of your established members depart, that there was something wrong with your organization. Also, you felt the same worry when your worship attendance first increased and then returned to the level you had had before the new members arrived. Actually, you still show a net increase of ten percent in membership and your established members still come to church, though a little less regularly. Your financial giving is up five percent and would be higher except for the loss of a few members who were large contributors. I suspect that many of you here are upset about the situation because of the close ties you had with the few members that left."

"So things aren't so bad?" one officer asked.

"What is bad is your current state of depression," Beth answered. "You failed to understand that an influx of new people with values a little different from your own was going to bring change."

"How are they so different?" Henry wanted to know.

"Not entirely different," Beth responded. "Just enough to make you feel uncomfortable without knowing why. The new members are better traveled, less traditional, and more questioning than your established members. They are less interested in denominational values and more interested in the application of general principles. They joined this church partly because their educational and economic backgrounds were similar to your own. They felt you would be more flexible than other churches because of your receptiveness to different ethnic groups. In fact, they still perceive you as being their best choice."

"I guess they should." Ralph Wesley, a teacher in the church school, spoke up. "Look at how we changed the worship service for them. And the church school classes will never be the same either. We don't have teaching sessions any more, just debates."

"Aha!" Beth smiled. "We have an honest man in the group. Most of you are careful not to express your resentment of the changes that have come about here. You prefer to repress it and show instead some free-floating anxiety over what the staff might do to bring your church back to you!"

"I don't appreciate that," said Bob Lindsey, the oldest and most respected officer on the board.

"What don't you appreciate?"

"You're implying we've lost our church. We still have our church."

"Not the way it was," Beth observed. "It's changed. Your worship service is different, your church school is different, and even your choir sings different songs. The church is people, and you have a large number of new people who are different."

"Well, we haven't changed completely," Bob argued.

"No," Beth agreed, "just enough to make you aware of a small headache that won't go away. But now if you can face up to what's causing your headache, maybe you can come up with a remedy—if everyone agrees with my diagnosis."

A moment of silence went by, and then some of the officers nodded affirmatively while others shrugged their shoulders and folded their arms. They talked among themselves for a while and then turned back to Beth. Paul Holtman took it upon himself to speak for the group.

"No argument here," Paul said. "Let's hear your solution."

"Well, the truth is I don't have a solution," Beth replied, "but I do have some suggestions. I believe that a more positive interpretation of what's going on should be made to the congregation. There's a lot to be said for an energetic church that doesn't repeat the same old things over and over. According to research, most people like to see themselves as innovators—whether they are or not. So a good PR job ought to include newsletter articles and announcements from the pulpit about the exciting new things that you are doing. Put the emphasis on what you are doing as a church, not on what the new people are making you do. You should express appreciation for the fresh new approaches your newer members have brought. Even if you have trouble buying into all that, start acting as if you do believe it and see what happens."

"I want to start with Ralph Wesley." Ruth Benson grinned. "He needs an attitude adjustment in the worst way. Listen, Ralph, a church school class *needs* discussion and debate. The members don't have a chance to do that at the worship service, and they learn better when they can voice their opinions freely. Why not build into your lesson plan some role play in which your combative debaters could participate? For example, have one of them play Moses and let the class question him about his attitude on what's going on today. I've seen some pretty interesting discussions generated from—"

"All right, all right," Ralph said. "I get the idea. Let's talk about it later."

"I know that you don't want to take up time talking about specifics here," Beth continued, "but Ruth has the right idea. Instead of complaining about the changes, see what you can do to make them work within the values of the church."

"What can you do about teenagers who hug and kiss in the church hallways?" Barbara Johnston asked. "There's a time and place for everything, but these kids don't seem to know it."

Henry spoke up. "Oh, you can do a lot with that. Ask Art to do a series on loving relationships."

"You mean *sex?*" Barbara sat up straight.

"Maybe, unless you have something against its being taught in church," Henry responded. "But start out with a look at relationships—what it means to fall in love. Art has some excellent material on that. And the best time to teach it is when you have a demonstrated interest in the subject."

"Well, I don't want Barbara to feel that she has to come to me for that," Art replied. "I'm sure she could handle the subject by herself."

"Uh—no, I think I would like some help," Barbara said.

"At any rate"—Beth addressed the group again—"this sort of frank discussion ought to go on all the time here. Before you do something new, discuss it with each other and see if it fits into the goals of your church. Try and get some mileage out of what these new members have brought you."

Another moment of reflective silence passed, and then Ralph Wesley summed up the feelings of the group. "Maybe," Ralph said, "maybe we haven't lost our church after all. Perhaps we are just seeing something a little different. It'll take an adjustment or two, but we may be better off for it in the long run."

"I'd go along with that," Bob agreed. "We still have our church. But when everything changes, we have to make some changes too."

After the meeting, Art invited Beth, Paul, and his associates to share a cup of coffee in a kind of post-mortem ritual.

Henry was so elated he couldn't contain himself. "Wow, Beth! I've got so many sermon ideas coming out of this meeting I don't know where to begin. You sure have made a big difference. For a while there, I was really worried. I held my breath when you told Bob Lindsey we had lost our church. Bob is one of the founders of First Church. I didn't know what he'd say!"

"Did you understand the technique or tactic that Beth was using?" Paul Holtman asked.

"No."

"It's called 'cognitive dissonance.' She put the group off balance by making a threatening alteration to their self-concept. And then she let them resolve the dissonance by accepting a new solution. She gave them the choice of resisting the change and getting stuck in the mud or accepting the change and making it fit into their values. And who wants to be stuck in the mud?"

Tactical use of cognitive dissonance

"Let me see if I understand that." Henry thought for a moment. "Cognitive dissonance creates some sort of imbalance?"

"You introduce an imbalance or a conflict into the self-concept," Paul replied. "Think of being pushed off a side-walk into the street. If it's a hard push, what would be your reaction?"

"I would resent it and jump back onto the sidewalk."

"Right. But what happens if it's a gentle push, as if it were for your own good?" Paul asked.

"Then I might stay in the street," Henry responded.

"Therefore, if I want you to go in a certain direction, I should apply just enough dissonance to be felt but not so much as to create a negative reaction," Paul concluded. "The 'push' in cognitive dissonance comes in the form of a verbal threat to what one thinks about oneself. You have to use the right amount of threat—not too much and not too little."

"So that's how cognitive dissonance works," Henry said. "I've got to give it a try!"

Beth laughed. "Whoa, Henry. It's one thing for an outsider like me to use that technique. It's another thing for an established leader to do it. You could come out a loser."

"What do you mean?"

"Often two things happen when a highly credible source, such as yourself, says something that threatens us. First, we may adjust our thinking in the direction you desire. But we also adjust what we think of you. You've done something to us, and we don't like you as much. You lose credibility, and it's harder for you to work with us on the next go-round. I can get away with it because people will figure I'm just doing my job. Besides, they won't have to put up with me any more."

"So the minister should never use cognitive dissonance," Henry concluded.

"Well, don't rule it out altogether," Beth replied, "just move slowly. A little dissonance works fine if you don't hit your members over the head with it. But I wouldn't try something as dramatic as you saw tonight. I may have pushed a little too hard. People will remember me for a long time. You don't want to be remembered that way. One minister told me it's the difference between a priest and a prophet."

"Sometimes a minister has to be a prophet," Henry objected.

"Yes, but we can mete out our prophetic utterances in incremental dosages." Ruth joined the discussion. "We don't have to score a touchdown with a desperation pass. We have time to march down the field."

"I can think of some exceptional times when a minister should do some brave speaking," Paul said. "But a high-threat message carries a high price. Usually, a mild threat works better and leaves the credibility of the minister intact. People respond more favorably if the message sounds like a helpful warning rather than a prophetic denunciation."

"The smart thing might be to bring in an outside prophet —like we did with Beth." Art smiled. "At least the church will still have its ministers to kick around."

"I'm confused about how cognitive dissonance as a tactic fits in with the strategies of compliance, internalization, and identification," Henry said. "I would think—"

Ruth interrupted. "Wait a minute. This discussion is getting too esoteric for me."

"Let me try to help," Paul responded. "Henry is talking

about three strategies that can be used to influence behavioral change. Compliance requires a concrete form of rewards and punishments—either you get the bonus or you don't. Identification is limited to a more abstract type of reward or punishment, to be liked or disliked. Internalization involves an abstract positive reinforcement, when we can agree on the content of what makes sense. Or we may experience a negative reinforcement when our beliefs do not agree."

"Let's get back to my problem," Henry said. "It seems to me that the tactic of cognitive dissonance we were discussing is just the applied form of compliance."

"A tactic is an operation to get what you want. Some people prefer the word 'technique,'" replied Paul Holtman. "Cognitive dissonance as a tactic can be used with all three strategies."

"But doesn't the application of cognitive dissonance carry reward-punishment with it? After all, a mild threat is a punishment. I thought that's how compliance works."

"Actually, reward-punishment is inherent in all three strategies," Paul explained. "Reward-punishment might be better understood in the context of positive and negative reinforcements. For example, in the identification approach, an expressed liking of someone often is a positive reinforcement."

"And avoidance behavior can be a negative reinforcement, but not always," Art said. "If a nagging person changes to simple avoidance, that can be a blessing. It really depends on the context and the relationship of the persons interacting. A parent who continually nags and then ceases to criticize may be perceived by the child as not caring any more. You have to know something about the personalities of the individuals to apply any strategy effectively."

"That's right!" Beth jumped into the discussion again. "Because a group is a collection of individual needs and values, I interviewed every member of your board as well as key members in your congregation so that I could anticipate their responses and get a picture of their values."

"I still don't understand Barbara Johnston," Ruth Benson mused. "Two years ago, she would never have objected to teenagers showing affection at church. To hear Barbara talk now, you would think that she was a retired spinster instead of a young, attractive television announcer."

How making sense works

"That was before Barbara went through her divorce," Beth replied. "I can say, without betraying any confidences, that this is a good example of what I mean by understanding individual needs. In fact, I was glad to hear Henry suggest that Art do a series in her class. Barbara thinks a lot of you, Henry. It wouldn't hurt for you to make a visit either."

"So we need to look beyond the content of what Barbara was saying. Part of her reaction came from personal problems," Henry observed.

"She may have identified the changes in her own life with the changes that the church is undergoing," Art said. "In psychological terms, the conflict of the church became an ink blot on which to project her own fears. That's not an unusual role for the church to play. Often a verbal onslaught on the minister comes from the same type of dynamic."

"After you look at individual needs, then what?" Henry wanted Beth to continue her explanation.

"Then you think about the cluster of values that the members of the group have in common," Beth responded. "If you want cooperation, it's best to concentrate on commonalities rather than differences—particularly when the situation is sensitive."

"What was the shared value that united us?" Art asked.

"You have a common pride in being members here," Beth replied. "As simple as that sounds, not all churches generate that feeling. So I knew a message directed to pride in your membership would be a good anchor. I also tried to appeal to a common pride in the ethnic mixture of your congregation, hoping your flexibility in that area would carry over."

"That's why you started off your presentation on such an upbeat note," Ruth Benson said.

"It was a safe point of departure," Beth went on. "As to my next step, I knew that an outsider with only one report to make would not find much use in the strategies of compliance and identification."

"So that left internalization," Henry said.

"Yes, I had to appeal to something that would make sense to the members of the board. That something was to convince them of the validity of change for the future. But since their future was clouded with doubt and apprehension, I had to do something to move them in the right direction."

"So you chose the tactic of cognitive dissonance," Henry observed.

"I wasn't sure how much to use," Beth admitted. "So I played it by ear and backed off when I saw some board members fold their arms and shrug their shoulders. I needed to deliver enough of a threat to get them off dead center, but not so much as to move them beyond what they could accept. Cognitive dissonance is like flying by the seat of your pants. It's not a precise technique."

"You played it well," Art said. "I like the way you allowed some face-saving toward the end—particularly with Bob Lindsey. He needed to come back and say that his church wasn't lost, after all."

"So to sum up," Paul concluded, "your overall plan was to create an immediate attitude change in the members of the board. To do that, you assessed the individual needs and values of the congregation and came up with a message appealing to a value held by us all. Then you focused on what might make sense to us in the future and sought to bring about an attitude change with cognitive dissonance. You kept quiet long enough to allow for some face-saving and also for the board members to interact and start thinking about solutions. And it should also be added that you laid the basis for this discussion with a careful definition of the problem."

"One other thing I'm concerned about is a previously held attitude that might reverse the change—such as resentment of new members by the old," Beth noted. "Any change that comes about suddenly is subject to reversal. And remember, it was the attitudes of the board members that changed, not those of the congregation at large. Furthermore, the strength of that change may not be as great as we hope. If you like what's happened, you will need to reinforce it with a redefinition of the situation in the pulpit, in church school classes, and in your newsletters."

CONCLUSION

In discussing these strategies for changing attitudes and behavior, we have been talking about what theorists call "behavior regulation." No one can regulate in the sense of actually controlling the behavior of another, short of using some very authoritarian methods. But as leaders, we want to take steps that will motivate persons to change their behavior in a way that will fulfill the purpose of our organization. This is the sense in which we are seeking to regulate behavior. Certainly, behavior regulation in churches is not control in any final sense. Even the best-laid plans for influencing behavior require constant attention and backup strategies.

Changes in behavior come about in two ways: (1) through targeting certain attitudes and (2) through targeting behavior itself by getting people to act in a certain way. Beth Lexington, as a visiting troubleshooter, advocated both ways. She worked first of all for attitudinal change in the leaders of the church through cognitive dissonance and then recommended specific behavioral reinforcements to develop change in the congregation. A planned change usually follows that pattern in churches, moving from the leaders to the members. But attitudinal change is not enough; behaviors must change, too, and develop into habits.

Henry learned the basic strategies for behavior regulation and some of the tactics used to implement these approaches. He also saw the importance of credibility in laying the basis of leadership. But a leader must be more than "believable" and "knowledgeable." A knowledge of managerial skills means very little if the skills cannot be applied to behavior regulation. If a minister wants to influence the members of the congregation and bring about change, an applied understanding of behavior regulation is vital.

One of the most complex areas where more than one strategy must be used is in community change. In this area, Henry next learns about the "diffusion process" and how change must be approached in stages.

4

A Community Change Strategy

Henry's favorite pastime on his day off was taking a bicycle ride with Janet. He enjoyed the changing of the seasons in the city park areas and the academic activity around the university. But the city was growing more crowded and traffic problems had doubled.

One day as Henry was peddling up a hill near the university, a pickup truck pulled out in front of him. Henry swerved and collided with the curb, skinning his knees and bending the front wheel of his bicycle. The pickup did not stop. Apparently the driver never saw him. Henry was furious; the city had to do something to ensure the safety of bicycle riders.

The next week, Henry described the incident to Ralph Wesley, who was on the mayor's commission for city planning. Ralph listened for a while, but his response was disappointingly indifferent.

"We've already heard from a delegation of university students about this problem," Ralph said. "As you probably know, the city has other worries bigger than bicycles."

"But surely putting in a few bicycle paths and establishing some routes along existing streets—"

"—would be a costly proposition. To do what the students asked would cost over two hundred thousand dollars."

"That seems reasonable."

"Not with our little budget," Ralph replied. "The city's broke."

"But there must be quite a few accidents involving bicycles," Henry said. "It could be a very serious problem."

Ralph smiled. "You sound like those students from the university. They didn't have any facts either."

"I know what it's like to be run off the road," Henry retorted. "And I'll bet those students do, too."

"Well, talk to *them*," Ralph said. "Maybe you can come up with something."

Henry did just that. He visited the office of the campus newspaper and found a receptive audience. The paper had carried several articles about the city's lack of concern for bicycle riders. But they had very little hope of changing things. The student editor, Jill Ferguson, explained the situation.

"We had a well-organized campaign," Jill said. "Over fifty students got together and protested at a meeting of the city council. But nothing happened."

"Did you present any statistics on bicycle accidents?" Henry asked.

"Unless there's a death, the police don't keep track of bicycle accidents," Jill replied. "Many of them go unreported. Did you report your accident to the police?"

"No."

"Even if you had, it wouldn't have been recorded," Jill continued. "No one really cares. It's the same old story—unless your group has power, you end up with zip."

About that time, a staff adviser, Dr. Ellen Seabrook, pulled up a chair and joined the conversation.

"I'm tired of hearing about how powerless you are, Jill," Dr. Seabrook said. "That's baloney! Students have a lot of power. You're supposed to be smarter than that."

"We've held meetings, written articles, and gone to City Hall. What more can we do?" Jill asked.

"You really don't know, do you!" Dr. Seabrook shook her head. "What did we talk about in political science last week? Sometimes I wonder why I bother to teach you people anything."

"Uh—well, we talked about diffusion," Jill tried not to look intimidated. "Is that what you're referring to?"

"Yes, that's what I'm referring to." Dr. Seabrook's tone was serious. "And guess what—you're going to take this bicycle problem and write a paper on the diffusion strategy—a *good* paper."

"I'd like a copy," Henry said.

Jill groaned. "Oh, no."

"I'll see that you get one," Dr. Seabrook promised. "Better yet, I'll mail it to you. Let's meet back here in one month and discuss it. We just might make this Jill's semester project, with the Reverend Mr. Whittimore assisting."

During the next month, Henry called the police department and found that Jill's facts were not quite accurate. The police did keep records of bicycle accidents when they involved serious injury. In fact, the police saw it as a growing problem and one of genuine concern. The number of serious accidents had multiplied by six in the past three years. Now there was one death every two months. The police chief had mentioned these statistics in a recent televised interview. And the television station had received a number of phone calls after the program aired. When Henry met again with Dr. Seabrook and Jill, he presented this information to them.

Dr. Seabrook's reaction was swift. "Obviously, you did not check the police records first-hand, Jill. You'd better not make that mistake when you start graduate school next year.

"Now, about your paper. You correctly outlined the diffusion strategy, and you did some imaginative work. I want you to follow up with a campaign that carefully implements your paper. This time, I don't want you to share ignorance with your fellow students in a brainstorming session. Brainstorming is only good when you are trying to motivate people; it's not a planning session. I'll lay down some definite guidelines and appoint some of your classmates to work with you."

"I'd like to help too," Henry said.

"Fine," replied Dr. Seabrook. "Let's go over Jill's paper and see where it takes us."

"I gather that diffusion is a strategy of stages," Henry remarked.

"That's right," Jill replied. "Diffusion moves from (one) spreading awareness of the idea, to (two) seeking information from opinion leaders about the idea and (three) trying the idea out and then (four) finally adopting or accepting the change."

Stages of diffusion

"Or you can think of these stages as levels," Dr. Seabrook added, "and make it simpler: First level, awareness through media; second level, interpersonal involvement through opinion leaders; third level, trial through experimenting and getting more facts; and fourth level, adopting the change."

"Apparently, these stages were derived from research," Henry noted. "They weren't just dreamed up by an armchair thinker."

"It all started out from studies in 1940 on agricultural innovations," Jill explained, "and then political science developed similar studies on voter habits during elections."

"Let's start with the awareness level," Dr. Seabrook suggested, "and show how it applies to what we are doing."

"All right," Jill said. "Awareness is developed by the media: newspapers, radio, TV. In our campaign on bicycle safety, people have to perceive the situation as a problem. Otherwise, nothing will happen."

Awareness through media

"Can the media create that perception?" Henry asked.

"That's debatable," Dr. Seabrook answered. "For an issue to become a social problem, there has to be widespread agreement. If only a few people think our city's neglect of bicycle safety is a problem, I doubt that a media campaign would make a difference. However, most of our students would define it as a problem and, apparently, so would the police. I think we have a cultural base to build on."

"Bicycle safety is an issue," Henry noted. "But the *problem* is the city's *neglect* of bicycle safety."

Dr. Seabrook agreed. "Yes, and it's the *problem* that we want people to focus on."

"Jill's paper suggests a way of doing that."

"Right," Jill said. "We launch a multimedia campaign, including our campus paper, videotape productions on the public access channel, letters to the city newspaper, and a door-to-door petition for the city council. After that, we go after the TV and radio stations for prime-time news coverage."

Henry beamed. "It sounds good!"

"It sure does," Dr. Seabrook said. "We'll know whether it's effective if it reaches the interpersonal level. People have to start talking about it."

Role of opinion leaders

"That's where opinion leaders come in," Jill pointed out. "We have to identify the individuals that people go to for information on traffic and road safety."

"According to your paper, you plan to do that when you go door-to-door with your petition," Henry said.

"Yes. We'll simply ask people, To whom would you go for advice about traffic and road safety?" Jill said.

"And then you'll compile those names and note the ones mentioned most often," Dr. Seabrook concluded. "After that, you'll visit the opinion leaders, present your facts, and try to gain their support."

"Yes, we'll want to do that before people start talking to them," Jill said.

"If you win over the opinion leaders, the rest of the campaign should be easy." Henry was beginning to believe that the diffusion approach might work.

"You'll have to keep up your media campaign in order to reinforce positive opinions," Dr. Seabrook cautioned. "Opinion leaders are the key, but your work isn't over until you've gone back to City Hall."

"Only this time, it won't be just students protesting to

the city council." Jill was excited. "We'll have grass-roots support, with parents and children going to the meeting too."

"It's going to take a lot of phone calls to get commitments to make that trip," Dr. Seabrook said.

"We'll do it!" Jill replied. "Just wait and see."

"Don't forget to have some printed facts to give the council," Dr. Seabrook added.

"I thought that Mr. Whittimore might help me do that." Jill looked at Henry.

"You can count on it," Henry said, "and I'll go door-to-door with you too."

In the days ahead, Henry observed that what Jill anticipated in her paper indeed occurred. For example, a few people immediately responded to the media campaign and became what diffusion research calls "early adopters." But most people seemed oblivious to what was going on. Some of Jill's helpers assumed from this response that the campaign was not going well. Jill knew better. Diffusion takes time before the majority of people start to take notice. Henry persuaded the television station that had carried the interview on bicycle safety with the police chief to rebroadcast the discussion. And he made sure that Jill's helpers were watching the repeat of this interview. It succeeded in picking up their spirits for the door-to-door part of the campaign.

The survey for opinion leaders turned up four names of people to whom those interviewed most often looked for advice about traffic and road safety. Jill was not sure how to solicit their support. She asked Henry how he would approach them.

"We should tell these opinion leaders the truth," Henry decided. "They should know that their names came up the most frequently in our survey as persons we should talk to. Since they have a reputation for being knowledgeable about safety, we can assume their interest. We can show them the information that we have on bicycle safety, and maybe they'll share some information with us."

"That's good for a start," Jill said, "but how do we close the deal and gain their support?"

"Probably the best strategy would be the it-makes-sense approach," Henry said. "Your teachers would refer to it as 'internalization.' We need to find out what makes sense to them about bicycle safety and go from there."

"Would you visit these opinion leaders with me and guide our discussion?" Jill asked.

Henry was flattered. "Sure, I'd be delighted to."

The first visit was short and to the point. The opinion leader quickly agreed that something should be done for bicycle safety and promised support. The second visit was with a middle-aged man, Charles Juniper, who had more than just a passing interest in the subject. Two years ago, his daughter had been seriously injured in a bicycle accident.

"My daughter went through three operations after her accident," Charles began. "I'll do anything you ask to get something done. Have the other people you visited shown an interest?"

"So far we have only visited Nancy Barnwell," Henry answered. "We still have Jim Callaway and—"

"Jim Callaway?," Charles interrupted. "You're going to visit Jim? Great! I've known that guy for years. I'll guarantee *his* support—no problem. Also, there's a bicycle club getting started on the other side of town, and I can give you a name to contact there. Who do you know on the city council?"

"We don't know anyone personally," Jill replied.

"Well, I know a couple." Charles grinned. "I'll talk to them and let them know that people are beginning to take a serious look at this issue. And about time, too."

"We thought we would write out some facts and—"

"You want facts on bicycle safety?" Charles broke in again. "I'll give you some. I've got information on what other cities have done."

"Terrific!" Jill exclaimed. "That saves us a lot of research."

"I want to see you come up with the largest group ever to appear before city council," Charles said. "Those politicos are impressed by numbers. They see votes. Are you going to develop a phone campaign?"

"Several students have volunteered—"

"Don't use students," Charles warned. "Use callers that other people might know. Let me help you organize your phone campaign. I know some people who owe me from stuff I did for them."

The next month, with Charles Juniper's help, over three thousand phone calls were made. People were beginning to take notice. At first, the members in Henry's congregation were amused and a little irritated by his involvement in the campaign. The city newspaper printed a cartoon of Henry on the editorial page, entitled "The Peddling Parson on Crusade." The teenage members in Henry's church loved it; others seemed embarrassed and worried about the image of First Church. One afternoon, church officer Bob Lindsey came to visit Henry.

"Of all the issues to get involved in!" Bob began. "Bicycle safety surely must take a back seat to poverty, race relations, child abuse, health problems—to name just a few! Where are your priorities?"

"I've been involved in those other issues," Henry protested, "but bicycle safety is such a simple, reasonable thing to ask for. It angers me that we haven't done something when so little is required to correct it."

"I suppose that's a good answer." Bob nodded in agreement. "But I hope it's not taking too much of your time. One thing that's in your favor is the kids in our congregation. They look on you as a cult hero. Certainly, the parents are not going to make too much trouble with their children behind you. You picked a safe issue."

"I felt kind of silly after seeing that cartoon in the paper," Henry confessed.

"It does give people something to talk about." Bob laughed. "Ralph Wesley clipped it out and put it up on the wall in his office. He makes jokes about your campaign, but I think he admires you for sticking with it. You're going to get some kidding, but I predict you'll come out ahead. You're doing something for our children and that's important—even if the issue isn't one of the top ten social problems."

"I suspect our board is relieved that I didn't pick one of the top ten," Henry observed.

"Probably so," Bob admitted.

It was true that the city's neglect of bicycle safety would not always occupy a number-one place in Henry's community outreach. But he was determined to see it through. As causes go, at least it was worth the small effort he had invested. If nothing else, the campaign helped Henry understand how community change comes about in a climate of relative indifference.

When Henry stood at the door after worship services, some of his members joked about the bicycle safety campaign. But a growing number congratulated him for taking part, and some even volunteered to help. Jill's paper on diffusion had predicted this sort of response. People at first are amused by an innovative

The interpersonal level

change, then they consider its benefits, and finally they adopt it. The campaign had successfully reached the interpersonal level. Most people not only were talking about it but were considering it.

The city council agreed to give the issue of bicycle safety a place on the agenda for their next meeting. Jill saw to it that the date of this meeting was widely publicized. She sent out a call for all concerned parents, students, and other interested parties to be there. When the big day came, the chamber was filled, with an overflow crowd standing outside the door. The council heard two hours of petitioning from the group, with individuals making impassioned speeches to loud cheers and applauding from the rest. The TV cameras were there, as well as representatives from radio stations and the press. Finally, the president of city council addressed the group.

"I cannot remember," the president said, "when an issue has caught fire like this one. You have presented your case well and documented your claims. I assure you that this council will start its own campaign for bicycle safety in our city. It's true that our budget is in bad shape. But if we allocate funds over a three-year period, we can do it. Working together with you, we *will* do it. I pledge to you my personal support, and I'm sure that the other members of council will do the same."

Final adoption

The delegation applauded, and Jill thanked the council for their support. The next day, the press announced victory for the bicycle safety campaign and printed a map of the proposed changes. Jill and Henry were both interviewed on local TV, and everyone treated the announced changes as if they had always supported them.

CONCLUSION

Our understanding of diffusion came from observing how new products and ideas gain public acceptance. Diffusion follows a standard cumulative normal curve, with early, middle, and late adopters. Most of us (68 percent) are not among the first or the last to accept change; we fall in the middle range. We become aware of an innovation through the media, get advice about it from someone we trust, try it out or evaluate its benefits, and then decide whether or not to accept it. But an idea that does not fall within our values in the first place is unlikely to be accepted, even with a good campaign.

Within the stages of diffusion, one will find the familiar interpersonal strategies at work. For example, both internalization and identification were useful in soliciting opinion leaders in Jill and Henry's campaign. The campaign made sense (internalization) to Charles Juniper because his daughter had been involved in a bicycle accident. Furthermore, Charles followed through with a phone campaign that relied on callers with whom people would identify (identification). Compliance was at work in convincing the city council members, who faced the possibility of losing votes if they did not comply with the wishes of a large pro-biker delegation. Attitudinal change will not occur without the incorporation of at least one of these three interpersonal strategies. Diffusion by itself is not enough to bring about change if one wishes to plan an outcome.

Opinion leaders carry a significant but very limited function of leadership. As information sources on specific issues, they may or may not be leaders in any other senses. The term "opinion leader" is jargon from research; it really does not tell us much about what it means to be a leader.

Perhaps formulating an encapsulated definition of leadership would be helpful in drawing together what has been said. Part of Aristotle's genius was in never giving a short definition to anything important. But if a short definition of the word "leader" could be inferred from his book *Rhetoric,* it would be that person who has discovered the available *means of persuasion* and knows how to apply them.

Today, these *means* are listed under strategies and tactics, and the art of persuasion becomes the social science of behavior regulation. We have seen how behavior regulation has three basic strategies: internalization, identification, and compliance. And we are learning how dissonance, social judgment, and reinforcement (reward-punishment) can be applied as tactics.

A leader must first be perceived as a credible source. Just as opinion leaders are considered credible within specific areas, a church leader must be perceived as trustworthy and compassionate within the church. After that, a leader becomes one who knows the nature of his or her organization and applies the appropriate strategies and tactics of behavior regulation. Other interpersonal skills are helpful too, but none are as important as behavior regulation. The key to successfully regulating behavior, of course, is versatile management. The leader must know *what* strategies to apply *when.*

THREE

Highland Church

5

Henry as Head of Staff at Highland Church

At the age of thirty-eight, Henry had mixed emotions about becoming head of staff at Highland Church. Although Highland was smaller and had fewer assistants than First Church, Henry felt that he had a lot to learn before taking such a position. At the same time, he did not know at what age he would learn enough to be a head of staff. Art Wellborn assured him that there was no age in which such enlightment would come. Heads of staff never know enough.

Henry had not sought to become a senior minister. His résumé was not in circulation at the time he was Art's associate, and he had no plans to move. But one Sunday morning when it was Henry's turn to preach at First Church, the Highland search committee was there to hear him. Unknown to Henry, both Jim Monroe and George Franklin had transferred to Highland, as a result of career moves that took them out of Eastwood. Even though Jim and George were not on the search committee, they were good friends of the chairperson, Colonel Bill Platitus.

After the service, Colonel Platitus met Henry at the church door and invited him and Janet to lunch. One thing followed another in the fashion of a whirlwind courtship with Highland, and Henry woke up one morning several months later still puzzled by his new surroundings. Perhaps some terrible joke had been played on him.

The one brief shining hour for some ministers may be in

preaching, for others in counseling or perhaps teaching or tending to community needs. But the largest number of hours are spent in meetings with committees, staff, officers, and other people involved in organization. Sometimes it is boring, routine work. Much like taking out the trash,

Staff leadership

it may not be something you enjoy but things get messy when you don't pay attention to it. Other times, more importantly, the feelings of people are involved.

At first, Henry hated and feared most of his organizational responsibilities. But he had one enduring trait that made him a better senior minister than he thought. Anything Henry feared became a challenge to him. As a child, he conquered his fear of lightning by reading everything he could find about it. When he understood it, he stopped hiding and watched thunderstorms with a new fascination.

For a while, it appeared that the two associates at Highland Church, John Thomas and Mary Duncan, got along well with each other, but then a storm began to brew.

Conflict management

Henry could feel the chill between them at staff meetings. Afterward, each one made a separate exit as if the other did not exist. Henry dreaded human conflict more than anything else. And so he began to look for ways of understanding it.

In Henry's files were résumés, letters of reference, and the notes taken by the personnel committee when each of the two associates was hired. Henry studied these documents to see if he might discover some psychological or sociological clue to their behavior.

Although everyone referred to John Thomas as "associate," he was not technically an associate minister. He was a student from a nearby seminary selected to work with Highland's visitation program. Henry hoped to keep him on staff during all three years of his schooling. In John's time as an undergraduate, he had been a psychology major, an outstanding athlete, and president of his fraternity. He had excellent recommendations from his professors at seminary, and everyone seemed to like him.

At Highland Church, John was showing a lot of good energy in personally visiting most of the congregation, and he had never missed a newcomer. People responded very positively to him and were helping him out in what he called the "committee chores." In fact, his visitation committee had caught some of John's enthusiasm and looked on their visits as fun. Henry paused as he read one of the notes taken by a member of the personnel committee: *If there is one thing that characterizes John Thomas, it is his love of people. He is a people-lover in every sense of the word.*

How in the world could a man like John Thomas have a falling out with anyone? Henry wondered.

Then Henry turned to the file on Mary Duncan, the associate in charge of church school education. Mary was a business major, a scholarship student at the top of her class, and had held a part-time job while in college. She was well-liked and respected by both classmates and professors. At seminary, she graduated cum laude and had superb recommendations from her internship, where she demonstrated "remarkable organizational skills."

At Highland, Mary had reorganized the church school so efficiently that problems were rare. Teachers were well trained, the departmental staff met regularly and kept things coordinated, and the resource center was cataloged and easy to use. Mary kept charts and graphs in her office that gave a clear picture of every aspect of the church school. No one doubted her competence, and people liked working with her.

Henry had been so impressed with Mary's organizational ability that he had asked her to work with John on the assimilation procedure for new members. And at first, both John and Mary had seemed eager to work with each other. What had gone wrong?

I have the best associates in my denomination, Henry said to himself. How could they not work together? It couldn't be jealousy—there's no lack of self-esteem. I could label it as a personality conflict, but what good does that do? What *kind* of personality conflict is it, and can anyone help?

When Henry went to bed that night, he dreamed of a large blackboard filled with personality types grouped in pairs. The first one was introvert-extrovert. "That one doesn't help," said Henry. "They both like working with people. Go on to the next."

"Dominant-submissive."

"Neither one of them is submissive. Hmm, I wonder if it's a power struggle. No, that doesn't fit either. Next?"

"Superiority complex–inferiority complex."

"Next!"

The list of personality types rolled on. Finally, Henry yelled out, "Stop! None of these are helpful."

The blackboard replied, "Describe what you know about them on the next line."

"Well, if I only have one line," Henry said, "write *John Thomas, people-lover* and *Mary Duncan, people*—uh, I guess she loves people too. But she's more of a people-worker. She gets work out of people. She's an organizer of tasks."

The board replied, "Task-oriented, person-oriented."

"All right, I've heard of that one," Henry said, "but so what? That describes them, but what can I do with it?"

The board made no reply, and the dream faded.

The next morning, Henry paid a visit to Dean Jim Monroe at the state university, where he was now head of the College of Social Sciences.

"I think everybody knows," Henry began, "whether they use the labels or not, that one of our associate ministers is task-oriented and the other is person-oriented. I thought that would be a great combination to work together, but I guess I was wrong."

"If you encouraged them to work closely with each other, you were wrong," Jim replied. "They live in two different worlds. John Thomas values feelings, expressive needs, and making people feel good. Mary Duncan finds satisfaction in making flow charts, interrelating tasks, and getting the job done efficiently. They have different goals, and one won't yield to the other."

"Should I get rid of one of them?" Henry joked.

Jim laughed. "We wouldn't want you to do that. The church is really benefiting from them both. Just stay out of their way and let them do their thing. They're both self-starters and should be treated as such."

"I'm not trying to be the big boss," Henry answered. "But I would like to end the cold war between them. Apparently, I started it when I put them on a project together."

"Probably so," Jim said.

"My immediate problem is that I'm required to do a job appraisal of my staff this month. What happens if one of them complains to me about the other? Do I shrug my shoulders and tell them to work things out the best they can? How can I repair the damage?"

"I wouldn't try too hard. You might exacerbate the situation out of your own anxiety. Why not let them learn from this experience, just as you have?"

"How?"

"Tell them how much you appreciate them both. Use a little scripture and talk about how we are blessed with different gifts. Why should a hand be expected to act like a foot?"

"You mean get them to appreciate each other," Henry said.

"Yes, but don't push it. You've got an ego-involved issue with a heavy anchor. Their positions won't change much. Move them along inch by inch. Don't shove them, or they'll go the other way."

"I think I'll start by pulling one of them off the assimilation project," Henry said.

"Good thinking," Jim replied. "But have them come together at your staff meetings, so that they at least can get a view of our total program. Coordination of efforts is still desirable even though joint projects may not be."

Later that day, Henry stopped by to visit Colonel Bill Platitus at the military base. Bill had not been as overbearing as Henry expected. In fact, Henry enjoyed talking to him.

"Tell me something," Henry asked Bill. "Wasn't it your idea to get the senior minister to do a yearly job appraisal of the staff? What did you have in mind?"

Staff evaluation

"Accountability," Bill answered. "You need it in churches just like anyplace else."

"Sure, but I want the associate ministers to feel like colleagues. I'm afraid that my doing a job appraisal will create the wrong climate. I don't want to intimidate them."

"Well"—Bill settled back in his chair. "Well now, it depends on how you do it. You could call them in and pronounce sentence on them with a list of strengths and weaknesses. That technique would put you at odds with them. Probably they'd go out and balance that scenario by telling some congregational member about *your* strengths and weaknesses!"

"That's what I'm afraid of," Henry acknowledged.

"Then don't do it that way," Bill said. "Instead, ask them to come in with a self-evaluation. Then sit back and listen to what they have to say about themselves. Add what you want and ask them if there is some way you can be of help to them."

"Hmm." Henry thought about it. "And that's accountability?"

"You bet it is," Bill answered. "The only accountability that's worth anything is when you encourage people to be accountable to themselves. It gives them a chance to analyze what they are doing in a more objective way than happens when they keep their self-evaluation private. And after they've had their say, they'll want to know what you think. Most of us really would like to learn more about ourselves and do a better job."

"Should I ask them to evaluate me?" Henry asked.

Bill smiled. "The personnel committee will evaluate you. But don't forget to ask your associates for suggestions on how you might work better with them. That would help resolve the dissonance created by your evaluation and give feedback that you need."

"You sound like you've been talking to Dean Monroe," Henry said.

"I sure have. We had a good discussion on this subject when it first came up before the board. We don't want the senior minister to alienate the staff with his job appraisal."

"I'm wondering how you'll evaluate me." Henry tried not to sound anxious.

"Oh, I wouldn't be too worried about that, Henry. You weren't chosen for this job on my say-so—even though I had already decided on you after talking to Jim Monroe and George Franklin. The board did a thorough investigation. For one thing, we like the way you ask questions, not of one person but of a number of people, before you make a decision."

"Why do you like that?" Henry asked.

"It shows you have a good intuitive feel for gathering information. Some executives will seek out only one likable source as a friendly sounding board for decision making. But you seek out sources from a number of circles in the congregation. That's good! It gives you a more accurate picture of what's going on. In effect, you are building a data base—or developing a pool of information on which to make decisions."

Developing a data base

"I hadn't thought about it that way," Henry said.

"You might even *improve* that technique," Bill continued.

"How?"

"Did you ever hear of opinion leaders?"

"As a matter of fact, I have."

"Then you know that opinion leaders have certain identifiable characteristics. They are gregarious, avid consumrs of media, and well traveled, and people usually think of them as competent in a specific area. In diffusion research, when people were asked to write down the name of someone to whom they would go for advice on new farming practices, the same name was mentioned over and over. Where there is such widespread agreement on a person, you have an opinion leader."

"I suppose you could get more than just one opinion leader in a given area."

"Yes, but usually each opinion leader will cover a different segment of the same subject. And these opinion leaders will be aware of each other and how they are related on that subject," Bill said. "When you ask about a different matter, you get different opinion leaders. For example, after the agricultural study, politicians became interested in opinion leaders. During elections, people seek advice as to the best candidate for the job."

"They go to opinion leaders."

"Correct," Bill replied. "In each community, there are opinion leaders who are sought out for advice on a specific subject."

"So you're saying that in our congregation there are opinion leaders to whom people go for advice."

"Exactly. And a wise minister might ask the members of the congregation to whom they would go for advice about the church school, or for whom they might vote on the board, or the hymns the congregation likes, or the type of fund-raising the congregation would respond to, or—"

"Or the type of approach to use for evaluating the staff," Henry interrupted. "Wow, that has a lot of implications. The minister who knows the opinion leaders really has a finger on the pulse of the congregation!"

"Now you've got the point. And a quick way to find out who are the opinion leaders is from the opinion leaders themselves. Usually, they are aware of the fact that people ask them for advice on a particular subject. If you ask someone, 'To whom do you go for advice on something?' and that person says that people often come to him or her

—then you probably have found an opinion leader."

"How many people do I contact before I have confidence that I have located an opinion leader?" Henry asked.

"That depends on the number of people involved in an activity or issue. Around ten or fifteen people might do for a question about church finance, with twice that many needed for a question about the church school. It's a simple procedure, not a real survey," replied Bill.

"So I don't have to hand out a questionnaire to the board to discover the opinion leaders. When something new comes up that we might want to do, I can just go to the people concerned with that issue."

"Right! You ask, 'Who do you go to for advice about—?' whatever. And it doesn't have to be something new. It can touch on any area in the life of the church. You'd be surprised to learn who the opinion leaders are. They're not necessarily rich, or members of the board, or well-educated. And remember, their competence will be in just one or two areas."

Later in the week, Henry propped his feet up on his desk and thought about the advice he had been given. Maybe, he thought to himself, a good leader is not someone who draws graphs and charts. The leaders Henry knew were more concerned about how information was gathered, the techniques used in making decisions, and people skills. The day before, when he brought his associates in for job appraisals, he felt comfortable in doing it. When Mary Duncan presented her self-evaluation, Henry had a framework in which to respond. He knew that Mary prided herself on enlisting people for tasks.

After she had finished, Henry asked, "How would you summarize your overall function at Highland, Mary?"

Mary paused for moment and then said, "I'm a coordinator, a facilitator for getting people working in the church school, and a supervisor of my departments."

"And you're good at it," Henry agreed. "I'm extremely pleased with the jobs that both you and John are doing."

Mary winced at hearing her name linked with John's.

"Thank you," she said, forcing a smile. "But I admit I'm a little confused about John's function."

"Oh, John has a job with a different emphasis from yours," Henry replied. "You might say he's in the business of developing a sense of community or fellowship. He was hired as a cheerleader, a comforter, an ambassador of goodwill."

"What does he do?" Mary asked.

"He gets people enthusiastic about their church, and he motivates them to care about each other."

"And he does this without any organization—just drops in on people and occassionally has a spontaneous meeting?"

"That's right." Henry laughed. "A good example of that spontaneity is what John does with the singles. Most of the time, their meetings aren't even on our calendar. They just meet when they feel like it, which is really quite often. It's sort of like a family dropping in on each other."

"I see those people meeting and I just can't believe it." Mary shook her head. "They decide to do something for the church without consulting anybody else. There's no delegation of duties, and no one knows what anyone else is doing."

"They just do it," Henry responded. "And sometimes it overlaps with what other people are doing. But I think that people enjoy seeing that sort of enthusiasm."

"Maybe so."

"Mary, in every organization there's some steam that's built up from alienation, frustration with the system, and feelings of unimportance. John takes that steam and puts it to good use."

"Like a valve on a pressure cooker," Mary said.

"That's it. Now you understand John's function—and he's good at it."

"All right, I can live with that understanding," Mary said cautiously, "but do I have to work with him?"

"No, you don't." Henry laughed. "I see no problem in

your not working together. But I do hope you see his value."

"Well, at least I see his *function*." Mary smiled.

Henry knew that Mary was not a hundred percent convinced, but he hoped that she would be less likely to criticize John within her own circle. After a period of time, Henry would know from the number of rumors in circulation whether the trust level between his associates had improved. Rumors are a reliable measure of a deterioration in trust. Unfortunately, no amount of preaching will stop rumors. A change comes only through an improvement of interpersonal relationships, and Henry understood that the process would be gradual.

When John Thomas came in for his job appraisal, it was easy to praise him for his visitation program. John thrived on compliments; they gave him the incentive to work even harder. However, criticism of any sort tended to enervate him. Henry had to move carefully in one area where John was causing a problem.

"You have terrific people skills," Henry told John. "I hesitate to suggest any improvements to you, because then the congregation might want you as senior minister instead of me."

"If you have any advice," John replied, "I want to hear it."

"Well, it's something so basic that probably you already know it. I don't want to insult your intelligence."

"Tell me!"

"All right, if you insist. It has to do with the difference between small interpersonal groups and formally structured, larger ones. I'm sure you learned all that in your psychology courses. You could look at our meetings with the church officers and your small group meetings and know the difference right away."

Interaction with officers

"I'm not sure that I do know." John was puzzled. "Is there something wrong that I'm doing in those meetings?"

"Well, let me think how to put this." Henry paused to find the right words. "Groups of nine and under allow for spontaneous discussions. People can talk whenever they please to whomever they please, and the more interaction with everyone participating, the better the group feels. John, you do a top-notch job with small groups. It's meant a lot to our church."

John smiled. "Henry, one thing I like about you is that usually you are direct and to the point. I learned in a communication course that when a subject is sensitive, people qualify what they say and skirt the issue. That's the way you're acting right now. Are you afraid I can't take criticism?"

Henry laughed. "I should have known better than to pussyfoot around a psychology major. Well, you put me at ease, and now I can tell you. You're lousing up my officers' meetings."

"How!" John exclaimed.

"Not deliberately," Henry replied. "You just enjoy getting people into an open interaction with each other. Whenever you make a report, you encourage a freewheeling discussion. It makes our meetings go on too long when we have thirty people trying to interact with one another. We lose track of what we are trying to do."

"How can you blame me for people wanting to interact with each other?" John asked.

"Oh, I know it's their fault too," Henry continued. "But you start it with questions such as 'How do the rest of you feel about that?' Or 'I wonder what the reaction of our congregation would be to that?' Those sorts of open-ended questions are very appropriate in a small group for stimulating discussion—but not in an officers' meeting."

"What would you say is the purpose of our officers' meetings?" John asked.

"It's to hear reports and vote on things that already have been thrashed out in small committees," Henry responded.

"So there's no time for honest interaction," John said defensively.

"Interaction of any sort must be limited in a group that large," Henry answered. "It's not just the formality of the group that makes a difference, it's the size. If you put thirty dots on a piece of paper and then draw lines between them to show everyone trying to talk to the others, you'll see the problem. Usually a few people dominate the discussion. That's why we use parliamentary procedure. In large groups, it gives us rules as to who talks when."

"I never thought about it that way," John agreed. "But what you've said makes sense."

Henry had learned something important about John, beyond the fact that he was sensitive to criticism. The best approach to influencing John was internalization, to "make sense" to him. John could take criticism if it fitted into what he perceived as logical. Of course, not everyone's logic is the same. The trick is to find out what makes sense to a particular person, not what makes sense in general. Henry and John shared similar values and educational experiences. Therefore, in "making sense" they had a common basis on which to build. Later, without forcing the issue, Henry would help John see how the church was benefiting from Mary Duncan's work.

CONCLUSION

Church leadership begins with the leader knowing how to gather and assess information. Some leaders, like Henry, may do the right thing intuitively without knowing why. But knowing why something works is important if the leader wants to build beyond that point. For example, Henry gathered information from the congregation by visiting a wide variety of people. That technique gives the minister a more accurate reading of the attitudes of the congregation than just visiting church officers or church school teachers.

It makes even more sense to identify and visit the leaders who shape the opinions of congregational groups. An accurate data base on what the congregation thinks and feels sets the stage for the minister to act as change agent.

For example, it so happened that Jim Monroe and Bill Platitus were the right people (presumably opinion leaders) with which to discuss the subject of staff leadership. If the information they furnished had not reflected the values and attitudes of the congregation, Henry would have been worse off than before.

Assessing information requires a consideration of the context, the people involved, communication principles, and an appropriate strategy if change is desirable. For example, it was not enough to know that a conflict existed within the staff or to feel a sincere concern for the opposing members. If left unchecked, a conflict between staff personnel easily can spread to the congregation, with people forming coalitions, and it would encumber the staff with lowered job satisfaction, decreased productivity, and win-lose games.

Henry identified the source of the conflict as differing values on how to work with people. He sought to contain it by eliminating joint projects that forced the two staff members to work together. At the same time, he tried to create a sense of mutual dependency by showing how a good job performed by one benefited the other. His technique of communication was essentially nonthreatening. No special meeting was called to "openly air differences" —a sure way of fanning the flames. Instead, Henry allowed the subject to come up voluntarily at the time of job appraisal. Henry allowed for differences and did not call on one to become more like the other.

Conflict can only be managed in a supportive environment. The reduction of threat, furnished by a manager appreciative of the opinions of subordinates, encourages self-expression and a decrease of emotional stress—essential ingredients to a climate of trust. Henry did not push for "promises to do better"; he settled instead for a slightly altered perspective of his staff people's value to each other. In a sense, he was opting for creative conflict without the staff feeling a loss of personal prestige.

As a manager, Henry at first seemed tentative, perhaps

hoping the conflict would dissipate by itself. Few interpersonal conflicts do. But finally, he employed an appropriate strategy and showed signs of becoming the best kind of manager—a versatile manager in a complex organization. The need for versatile management becomes increasingly important to Henry as head of staff at Highland.

6

A Compliance Strategy

One of the times Henry enjoyed most during his daily work routine was his midday chats with Eleanor Peabody, the church's senior secretary. Eleanor was old enough to be his mother and no less nurturing to practically everyone who came into the office. She was a highly personal manager to the office workers under her supervision. She tended to exchange large amounts of information with the others, including personal opinions about the value of the work received. She liked others to participate in even the smallest decisions about office procedures. Whenever there was a conflict, which often happened among the secretaries, Eleanor would hold out for a win-win solution —or at least a good compromise with each party giving up a little (lose-lose). Since the office rules were always flexible to meet the needs of office personnel, new problems and solutions constantly emerged.

Eleanor spent a lot of time in motivational pep talks, getting the workers to share how their religious experience applied to their work. She frequently took time over the phone to counsel members who had been ill by suggesting remedies for taking better care of their health. Often, she had lunch with old-guard members and sang the praises of Henry P. Whittimore. Henry loved Eleanor and was very sorry to see her retire.

The new chairperson of the personnel committee, who would organize the search for a replacement for Eleanor Peabody, was George Franklin. Henry was stunned when

George told him that, instead of a "senior secretary" in the mold of Eleanor Peabody, the committee would be looking for a highly professional office manager who could handle the growing administrative responsibilities of the church office and day care center. The salary would be significantly increased, under the proposal of the personnel committee, and strong business credentials were preferred.

Henry feared that George Franklin's background as an oil company executive was contaminating the decision as to the type of person needed. Since the proposal of the personnel committee constituted a radical change in hiring requirements, the board voted to delay a final decision until a second meeting on the matter. After the first meeting of the board, Henry insisted that George join him for the customary cup of coffee with other officers at their designated restaurant. Henry was sure that, with the help of others, he could bring George to his senses and get him to withdraw from the position of the personnel committee.

"George," Henry began cautiously, "do you remember the discussion we had long ago, back at Eastwood, concerning the church and the nature of its organization?"

"I sure do, Henry." George gave him a mischievous smile. "It was a real eye-opener for me. As a matter of fact, what we discussed had a direct bearing on the decision of the personnel committee."

"It wasn't the decision I anticipated," Henry said.

"Now why is that?" asked Jim Monroe.

"I thought we agreed that the church is characterized by personal need fulfillment," Henry replied. "Its major approach is identification, and Eleanor Peabody was the embodiment of that principle. Why are we forsaking that?"

George laughed. "I love it! I've finally got Henry P. Whittimore in an indefensible position. You don't know how long I've looked forward to having this discussion."

"What are you talking about?" Henry was thoroughly puzzled.

"Henry," George responded with relish, "you've made

the mistake of taking a major approach and turning it into the *only* approach. If you remember our discussion on organizations, you will recall that *versatile* management is the key to any organization. The church is not exempt."

"He's got you, Henry," Jim said.

"Yep, it's point, set, and match," another officer agreed.

"What on earth is going on here?"

"I think we're about to see a validation of the compliance strategy at Highland Church." Jim grinned. "And after talking to George, I couldn't agree more."

"Hey, you people have been talking behind my back," Henry complained good-naturedly.

Jim nodded. "You're right, we're guilty."

"All right, you've got it figured out among yourselves," Henry acknowledged. "How come you didn't include me in your deliberations?"

"Suppose we had, and you agreed with us," George replied. "What good would it do you to back an increase in our office wage scale and a changeover from the Peabody personal-manager style?"

"You'd make a lot of enemies, Henry," Jim said. "Better stay neutral on this one."

"I don't like this change," Henry said. "And I don't understand why you all agree with it."

"Jim, give Henry a lecture and open his eyes." George reveled in his moment of victory.

"Well, at long last George Franklin is seeing all his treasured techniques from the oil company put to work in the church," Jim began. "We have an application here for management by objectives, time management, and all the other variations derived from the so-called school of scientific management. That sort of structuring allows for a reward-punishment tactic to work in a compliance strategy."

"It works whenever you need to structure authority and control is the issue," George responded.

"Is that what we're getting into? Why? How?" Henry was growing anxious.

"First of all, let's take a look at the Eleanor Peabody era of twenty-five years and the personal-manager type in general," Jim said. "Eleanor certainly was a personal manager,

| Personal vs. professional manager |

encouraging people to work from inner motivation. In essence, she was saying to our office personnel, 'Your pay may be low but your commitment to the organization is what matters. Your reason for working here must come from the heart, not the pocketbook. And I, Eleanor, will help you by meeting your needs of satisfaction, security, and esteem.'"

"What's wrong with that?" Henry asked.

"If Eleanor were hired as an associate minister in congregational care, nothing," Jim answered. "But she was hired to get out the paperwork from our staff, our board, and our committees. Our committee chairpersons were always complaining that things were never out on time. We didn't complain too loudly, because everyone loved Eleanor. And of course the work coming directly from the senior minister was done promptly. That way she had your backing, Henry. You two were constantly praising each other, and none of us here wanted to make trouble."

"I'm very unhappy that you didn't come to me about these problems," Henry said.

"Your only alternative would have been to dismiss Eleanor," Jim observed. "Would you have wanted to do that?"

"Well, no. I guess I see what you mean. But aren't we going to the other extreme by looking for an unfeeling, money-motivated, office manager?"

George spoke up. "He doesn't have to be unfeeling."

"He?" Henry exclaimed. "You're ruling out women? That's sexism!"

"Uh—well, one of our top candidates is a man and the other is a woman. We were going to let you choose between the two." George was embarrassed.

"Henry, you're too emotionally involved in this thing," Jim noted. "All we're saying is that we're tired of an inefficient office and we want somebody to run it right. The personal-manager type was OK when our church was smaller, but not now. We need a highly professional manager, one who greets people politely but doesn't stay on the phone all day. We're not going to take an unfeeling person, but we're going to make the salary attractive enough to get what we want. This job requires someone with advanced skills in office management. The extra money is in recognition of the fact that this office manager is very important to us. We're paying this person a good salary for the same reason that we pay you one, Henry."

Now Henry was embarrassed. He still wasn't sure he would like the change, but he agreed to go along with it.

At the next board meeting, the vote was unanimous in favor of the new hiring procedures of the personnel committee. After careful deliberation—five minutes—Henry chose the female candidate, Carol Berger, for the position of office manager. Carol was a stylish brunette with an air of confidence and efficiency. She gave straight, direct answers to questions regarding her competency. She offered very little information about her personal life.

Under the new procedures, Carol had control of the hiring and firing of office personnel. She replaced one person after two weeks. When someone asked her why, Carol simply stated, "We need someone with better computer skills to do the job." And that was that. A noticeable change to greater efficiency came over the rest of the employees. At first, Carol communicated with short memos, accompanied by brief verbal explanations. Later, when she learned the strengths of each worker, she held one-hour staff meetings on the second day of each week and made specific assignments. She met with Henry on the first day of the week to determine priorities.

Henry was amazed at the increased output of the office, and all seemed to be going well. But one day Carol expressed some dissatisfaction to Henry regarding his practices in communicating with the office staff. She was polite, but she made no bones about it.

"Henry, there are three things that I would appreciate

your considering in order to keep things running smoothly in the office," Carol began.

Working within a compliance setting

"I'd be glad to help in any way that I can," Henry answered agreeably. "You do excellent work."

"Good. First of all, your priorities change so often that it confuses my staff and lowers morale," Carol said.

"Is there any way you could pull together what you want so that we could finish one thing before starting another?"

Henry was indignant. 'I didn't realize I changed my priorities all that often, Carol. Could you give me an example?"

Carol showed Henry a list of her assignments, all neatly dated with the times that the staff began working on them. She pointed out how three of these assignments were radically altered by Henry after several days of staff work.

"Well"—Henry laughed—"I should have known that you would have things carefully documented. Are you going to turn me in to the personnel committee for inefficiency?"

"I like to follow procedure," Carol replied without smiling. "It would not be appropriate for me to go to the personnel committee before coming to you. I would never do that. But I do feel we have a problem."

"I'll do my best to correct it," Henry responded. "Now, what are your other suggestions?"

"When you have a job for us to do, how about giving it directly to me?" Carol asked. "It's hard for me to regulate our office schedule when our secretaries show me work that you've given directly to *them*. It throws our workload out of kilter."

"What happens in an emergency when I need things done right away?" Henry objected. "I've always taken work to the person I know can handle it."

"You've seen my schedule of assignments," Carol replied matter-of-factly. "I have to know what's happening and when, in order to run an efficient office. It won't take long to reassign duties when an emergency arises."

"Well, uh"—Henry dropped his head—"I'll have to think about it. I'm not sure."

"I see," Carol said quietly.

"What's your other suggestion?" Henry asked.

"Are you sure that you want to hear it?" Carol looked straight into Henry's eyes.

"Go ahead." Henry felt tense.

"Those after-lunch chats that you have in the office with our workers consume too much time and detract from what we're doing."

"Carol"—Henry leaned back in his chair—"I enjoy a family-type atmosphere. I feel that it's important to have a friendly relationship with my staff."

"Sure, I don't have any problems with that—but there's a difference between five minutes of friendly talk and forty-five minutes," Carol replied. "It backlogs our workload and gives the impression that our time isn't worth much."

"I don't know, Carol." Henry paused and deliberated. "I'm really not comfortable with any of these changes."

"Then I guess I've said enough." Carol dismissed herself politely and went back to her desk.

Two weeks later, George Franklin burst unannounced into Henry's office. He stretched his lanky frame over Henry's desk and started yelling.

"What in the—oh, I can't say it in church! What's going on with you, Henry? Are you crazy?" George's face was crimson.

Henry pulled back. "George, the only thing I know for sure is that you've had onions for lunch."

"You're not funny, Henry, not one bit." George sat down. "We get a super office manager, and now she tells me she's thinking of resigning. It took me a while to get it out of her but I found out why. Carol's quitting because of Henry P. Whittimore and his stupid treatment of the office. Why won't you let people do their job, Henry? What's your problem? I'm not just angry—I passed that stage six hours ago. I want to be polite to you because of what you've meant to our congregation. Basically, people respect your leadership. But you don't know how hard our personnel committee worked. And now you're dumping it down the drain!"

Henry paused for a minute and tried to collect his thoughts. He felt both guilt and anger; he wasn't sure whether he was right or wrong—or both.

"George, I need some time to think," Henry said slowly. "Could you convince Carol to stay on a little longer until we've had a chance to talk things out?"

"You mean with Carol?" George asked.

"No," Henry replied, "I mean with you and some other officers. I'm not used to the way Carol does things, and I need to understand how these new procedures are supposed to work. Could you buy me some time?"

"If you would come down off your high horse and let Carol run the office the way she needs to, maybe." George glared at Henry.

"All right, let's get together for lunch tomorrow," Henry replied. "Don't go bad-mouthing me. I'm not beyond redemption. I've even confessed to sin on occasion."

"I want to see you *correct* your sins," George said.

Henry invited Mary Duncan and Jim Monroe to have lunch with him and George Franklin and evaluate how things should be handled in the office. Henry began by giving an honest account of his conversation with Carol. He stopped when Jim Monroe started laughing.

"I can't believe that you find this matter a problem, Henry," Jim said. "Why can't you let Carol run her own show?"

"It's my show too!"

"When it comes to the office," Jim replied, "there's a difference between running the show and being a good manager. Carol was hired to run the office, just as Mary Duncan here was hired to run the church school. Your job, Henry, is to be a good manager."

"I don't understand," Henry said.

"Why is it that you don't understand?" Mary asked. "When it comes to the church school, you don't circumvent me by going directly to the teachers. Why can't you

**The role
of manager**

channel information through Carol instead of going around her and giving it to the secretaries?"

"They're my secretaries too," Henry complained.

"You really have an ego problem." George put his arm around Henry. "Are you jealous of Carol?"

"I don't think that's it," Jim said. "Henry is accustomed to the Eleanor Peabody era when the office was run like a pot-luck supper. He misses the fellowship."

"That's right, I do," Henry said. "I don't like the church becoming coldly efficient."

"Well, you better start—"

Jim interrupted George. "Go easy on Henry. He's had a hard time. He discovered the importance of liking relationships, and now he wants to apply that strategy to everything."

"I guess I'm still not convinced that compliance is the best strategy for our business office," Henry said.

Jim took up the challenge. "All right, you already know that compliance is a production-oriented strategy with limited utility. It does not work in churches among colleagues of equal status, such as among our board members. It will not work at pot-luck suppers or at your home Bible study. But when you have role specialization with managers and subordinates and behaviors that are concrete, measurable, and easily defined—then compliance may be your most efficient strategy."

"No maybe about it," George injected. "It is the *most* efficient strategy—given those prerequisites."

Jim grinned. "Well, it quickly can become inefficient when employee needs, such as rewards, are ignored and behaviors are not consistently monitored by managers."

"I think Carol has enough sense to give raises and keep sharp watch of her subordinates," George said.

"Rewards also include verbal recognition of accomplishments," Jim continued, "and consistency means adherence to a written procedure for what's right and what's wrong."

"It sounds like a system for fixing the blame on subordinates when productivity is low," Henry remarked.

"Quite often, managers react just that way," Jim responded. "Of course, the blame could just as easily be assigned to poor managerial planning and policy implementation. I hope Carol will sense that a church environment requires a more participative approach, with employees planning some decisions with her."

"Aha!" Henry exclaimed. "I like that! A participative approach means that both achievement and failure are shared."

"Yes, but role specialization means that participative decision making is not always desirable," George said. "Each employee has to be accountable within a specific area."

"That's true," Jim agreed. "You can't switch over to a total internalization strategy and maintain efficiency. But participation in lower-level decision making improves communication. And some employees need to feel included more than others. Remember, a good supervisor is a versatile manager. Compliance still is the logical strategy for our office, but the needs of employees cannot be ignored."

"How do I fit into this picture?" Henry asked. "What does it mean on my part to be a good manager in a compliance approach?"

"Treat Carol as a highly trained specialist," Jim answered. "She has skills you don't have. If you want an efficient office, let her run it. Your job is to describe the work that the senior minister wants accomplished. That means some careful organization of priorities on your part with the deadlines that you face."

"In other words," Henry remarked, "Carol was right to complain about my changing priorities."

"All of us occasionally have to change priorities," Mary said. "But when you do it several times a week, the office staff goes crazy. There's nothing worse than wasting energy on a job that didn't need doing in the first place."

"I must admit," George said to Henry, "you have real fortitude for letting your associate in on this discussion. Maybe you're not as insecure as I thought."

"I respect Mary's judgment, especially on business matters," Henry replied. 'She has some training that I don't have."

"The same thing is true with Carol," Jim responded. "Start treating her that way and see what happens."

"What else should I do as Carol's supervisor?" Henry honestly wanted to know.

"Think of yourself as a *manager,* not a supervisor," Jim continued. "A manager coordinates the overall organization and leaves the running of organizational units to supervisors. Again, let Carol supervise the office. Everything she told you is basically correct. Don't circumvent her. Give her the assignments and let her pass them on to the office personnel. It's not just a matter of disrupting her scheduling. When you go around her, it discredits her authority."

"I hadn't thought about it that way," Henry said.

"The same thing's true with your after-lunch chats," George noted. "When you consume too much office time with task-irrelevant behavior, you're shooting down her discipline."

"I guess I've made things pretty hard on Carol," Henry confessed.

"What bothers me is how you can regain Carol's trust," George reflected. "Usually when an employee such as Carol threatens to resign, trust is so violated that it's best to let her go. I just hate to see that happen."

"So do I," Henry agreed.

"George is right," Jim said. "A high threat from an employee, such as resignation, poses some special problems that we may not be able to overcome. Even if Henry does change his ways, Carol may not perceive it as a good sign. She may think that Henry has been coerced into accepting her demands and is lying in wait ready to get back at her."

Mary laughed. "Is that what you are doing, Henry?"

"Of course!" Henry grinned. "Seriously, I think the church has a special grace in these situations, and I would like to see it work out."

"If you do try to restore the relationship," Jim said thoughtfully, "do it with gradual reciprocal increments."

"I can't wait to hear what *that* means." George scratched his head.

"It means don't rush in with a bunch of gushy sweet talk," Jim replied. "When a relationship has been seriously disrupted, restoring it has to be a two-way street. You have to do it gradually, putting out a small positive stimulus and waiting to see if the other person responds in kind. If the offended party doesn't reciprocate with a positive response, you still have a problem."

"Does anyone understand what Jim's talking about?" George asked.

"Sure." Mary spoke up. "You give a little bit and see if the other person gives too. If it works, you've got the beginning of a new relationship that you gradually build onto from there."

"But don't do anything too magnanimous," Jim counseled. "People don't trust overnight changes when there's been conflict. Let Carol feel that she is slowly winning you over. That way, she is more apt to encourage you with little positive acts of her own."

"And the relationship becomes two-way." Henry liked the idea.

The next few months, Henry felt like a changed Ebenezer Scrooge. He enjoyed watching Carol watching him to see what he would do next. Henry started out by telling Carol he would try to honor her requests, with the caveat that he might slip up occasionally. Then he developed the habit of writing down his priorities and giving Carol a copy of them at the beginning of each week. When an emergency came up, he immediately called Carol into his office and asked her advice as to how it might be handled within her schedule. He was polite to the secretaries but only talkative when he took the staff out for an inexpensive lunch once every two months. And he was careful to limit this event to one hour. One day, Carol asked to meet with Henry after office hours.

"Henry," Carol said, "you're good with people. I have a problem with one of our secretaries that I don't know how to handle. This person started off very efficiently on our word processor. She obviously has good abilities, but now her productivity is lagging. I don't want to get into her personal problems—if that's what's bothering her. As to what I *should* do, I'm at a complete loss. I can't let her go on this way."

"Maybe you don't have to know her personal problems in order to help her," Henry said.

"Then what should I do?" Carol asked.

"You might start out with a simple principle from organizational research," Henry replied. "Everyone has a need to be included in the thinking-out part of the job as well as the doing."

"What's the application?" Carol wanted to know.

"Well, you might try sitting down with this person occasionally and including her in lower-level decisions that pertain to her role assignments."

Carol frowned. "What good would that do?"

"Maybe it would give her a feeling of more worth than just a button pusher," Henry said. "It's one thing to be told what to do. It's another to be included when decisions are made about how something should be done. She may be the type of person who likes to think about how her work might better be produced."

"And this would let her know that we value her opinions and want to include her in decisions affecting her work," Carol said thoughtfully. "All right, I'll try that."

Carol wasn't sure how to encourage creative decision making in word processing. But she started out by asking what programs might be added to the system to make it more efficient. To Carol's surprise, the young woman talked nonstop for ten minutes about a new program with an electronic dictionary that simplified spelling checks. The program was ordered and other employees began to make suggestions about improvements in their areas. As a result, Carol became more participative in her approach and often consulted Henry about employee suggestions. Increased morale and a good working relationship with Henry soon followed.

CONCLUSION

There are enough unhappy endings in the world without dwelling on their possibilities here. Suffice it to say that if the relationship between Henry and Carol had remained uncomfortable, Carol's resignation should have been accepted. Unhappy employees tend to become saboteurs. Churches often get into more trouble than corporations by assuming that time will heal all wounds. Time alone won't do it, and even the best interpersonal tactics sometimes fall short.

Compliance is the hammer in the organizational toolbox. Some managers use this tool exclusively, driving their point home: You will do as I say because I have the power to reward or punish you. At times, participative management is added as a motivational incentive to encourage job satisfaction. Compliance works if the tasks are observable and easily defined in a system with managers supervising subordinates. Continual monitoring also is necessary, with consistent rewards and punishments.

Probably the church will find limited application of this strategy but it is worth keeping in mind, especially in larger organizations where roles are delineated more clearly. Compliance furnishes a logical context where management by objectives, time management, and the like can develop efficiency. However, an efficiency technique that is imposed upon employees also can lessen both motivation and productivity. For this reason, newer forms of management are experimenting with motivational approaches to promote efficiency rather than forcing employees to comply with a rationally structured technique handed down by the manager.

Although efficiency is often linked with effectiveness in the compliance strategy, such is not the case with identification and internalization. People skills in churches usually cannot be measured by behavioral objectives. Efficiency and effectiveness are not always the same.

Some senior ministers may wonder whether compliance can or should be used with associate ministers. If the situation is similar to Henry's, probably not. The performance of his associates is not based on office efficiency or getting out a measurable product, such as paperwork in the office. As with Henry, their effectiveness depends on how well people like and trust them.

Also, it is doubtful whether Henry would be able to monitor constantly the activities of two innovative and energetic associates. And if such surveillance were possible, creativity and initiative would suffer. If independent thought is desirable, a manager cannot command obedience at the same time.

Again, compliance is best used with well-defined and routinized roles where expectations are clear-cut. For example, a sergeant will charge up a hill on orders from a lieutenant—no questions asked. Few churches will have an organizational structure with lines drawn that clearly. Also, seminary training encourages ministers to internalize values and to act out of a mature conscience. In a profound sense, their motivation is intrinsic; they look for a feeling of accomplishment within their own values of right and wrong. If an order violates their sense of integrity, they are not apt to carry it out. With most associate ministers in a democratic society, either the hill to be charged has got to make sense or the senior minister must be highly trusted as a wise and ethical person.

In general, the best approach for a senior minister is to

promote an environment where the ministers trust and respect each other and their competencies. If compliance is expected in a particular church within certain areas of the minister's work, then participative management often is the key to meeting this need. In any event, the senior minister should take time to learn the values of the associates and develop liking relationships within the staff.

One final link should be made in a book on leadership in the church—the use of media for extending the influence of the leader. Some people speak of media strategies as if media had some peculiar ways of influencing people above and beyond interpersonal strategies. Such is not the case. And yet, even though the strategies are not new, media do have particular techniques and functions in their channeling of messages. Because people attribute so much importance to the media as a source of information, they have power. As a leader, Henry was soon to discover how the uses of media could expand his own influence.

7

The Uses of Media by Church Leaders

Henry sat in his office and thought very hard about how to use the small amount of funds allocated in the church budget for advertising. He could not think of a single instance where a church with a modest advertising budget had made any impact at all. How should a leader recommend the use of these funds to the members of the board? Should the money be spent on radio, TV, or newspaper ads?

Certainly the budget would not go very far on TV, given the high cost of advertising. Was TV that much better than other media? Henry tried to think of someone who had the expertise to advise him in this area. The members of the board already had declined comment and left the matter to the pastor's discretion.

About that time, Henry received an invitation to a media seminar sponsored by the Ministerial Association. Through the city franchise, the cable TV company had made available four public-access channels. One of these channels carried local religious and health programming at no cost. The religious organizations, through the Ministerial Association, had developed a TV studio and hired a director, Ed Winters, a crusty retired media professor from the university.

Ed reportedly had been a favorite among his students and was notorious for using encounter tactics in his lectures. He particularly loved to argue with religious leaders, and it came as a surprise to some to learn that he was an active church member. Those ministers who had taped programs in the new studio spoke very highly of Ed and were eager to attend his seminars. Henry read the invitation over again and, after noting that the first lecture was on media impact, decided to attend. He found that Ed, living up to his reputation, was on the attack.

"Ministers think of media, especially television," Ed began, "as a powerful giant that reaches out into the living room of the viewers and snatches away their values. Violence! Sex! 'Oh, my goodness!' the minister says. 'How will I protect the families of my congregation? If only I had a chance to put *my* message on television, I could correct this evil.' Hogwash! The giant is a one-dimensional creature with much less power than you suppose. And the type of religious programming I see you doing would have no influence on anyone except a few of your own members. You're boring. You use no imagination, and most of you are wasting precious time on the access channel!"

| Effects of media |

As usual, Ed had baited his audience, and everyone started talking at once. No one disliked Ed; he was very helpful in training members of their congregations in the use of the studio. They experienced the same pleasure in debating him as did his former students.

"If we're boring, maybe you'd better train us better," one minister objected. "That's what we're paying you for."

"I've tried to tell you," Ed replied. "Don't do one-person shows starring the minister. Even Charlton Heston and Raquel Welch would be boring if they talked solo for thirty solid minutes. Get some variety. Bring in children to talk with. Do a role play, have a panel discussion, bring some visuals, present some music—don't just preach to us! You may do better in church but you have no sizzle on TV!"

"I think you grossly underestimate the power of TV," another clergyman said. "It does have an influence. Our members constantly complain about what comes into their homes. They can't keep track of what their children watch."

"Oh, sure, it has an influence," Ed responded. "Anything that you see and hear has an influence. But just how strong is it? Advertisers go crazy trying to come up with something that has an impact. They've tried subliminals, sex, hi-tech visual imagery—everything. And they're not at all satisfied with the results. According to research, TV ads help make people aware of new products and reinforce the use of old ones. Car commercials, for example, have an impact mostly on people who own that car already. So TV makes us aware and reinforces old habits. Outside of that, the research has come up with zilch. So much for your giant."

"But surely the effects on young children—"

"—are negligible compared to the effects of parental attitudes," Ed broke in. "Except for very disturbed children, the studies show no increase in violence as a result of watching violence. And a lot of university studies have been done."

Henry spoke up. "I'm not sure I believe those studies."

"Believe what you want," Ed said. "I'm telling you that an enormous amount of money was spent on studies in the fifties and again in the seventies. And the results were what I told you: awareness and reinforcement with no evidence of attitude change. Now I will admit that these studies were not equipped to deal with long-range effects. There may be a shaping effect with enough repeated messages. But we don't know that for sure. There are too many intervening variables to make a longitudinal study."

"Well, I believe it has an effect," another minister replied. "TV is on for eight hours a day in most homes, with seventy percent of people using the tube as their only source of news information."

"But suppose the studies I cited are right," Ed continued. "What does it say about your performance on TV?"

"I have people come up to me and say how much they enjoyed my program on the cable," a clergyman said. "And some of these folk I've never seen before."

"All right." Ed smiled. "There is some evidence that repeated TV exposure increases credibility. That's a plus, as long as you aren't boring. And that would expand your influence in the community. It gives your church visibility and helps people to become aware of what you stand for. Awareness is the first step to making a change in people. It won't create the change, but it gives you a start in the right direction."

"How would you build on it?" Henry asked.

"First, I would want to enlarge on the awareness factor," Ed replied. "TV is the most powerful tool for that because it combines sight with sound. Most people are visual; they believe what they see before they respond through any of the other senses. You can build on that with a multimedia approach. Put the same message on the radio and in the print media. Get all the senses working for you and let the law of repetition do its thing. If you can, give a new twist to your message and let people respond to a phone number. If the old, old story doesn't sound fresh, you won't get a response."

"If people don't talk about it, you won't get a response either." Henry was thinking about the diffusion process.

"That's true," Ed agreed. "But don't put the cart before the horse. First get out an innovative approach to your message that really grabs people's attention. Then go for the interpersonal response through phone calls, door-to-door visits—or perhaps by starting a small-group study."

"How do you know if you've gotten people's attention?" one minister asked.

"Do a survey in your own denomination. I'll help you with the random sampling," Ed answered. "Send out letters with a return-addressed card, asking: *(a)* Did you see such-and-such program? Yes / No *(b)* Did you like it? Yes / No *(c)* Did you tell anyone else about it? Yes / No. Send it out twice to get a good response. At least you'll know whether or not you're just spinning your wheels."

"A one-shot program wouldn't do any good," Henry noted.

"No, it wouldn't. The program has to be an ongoing series. You can't tell anything with just one show, especially on cable-access TV."

"One thing that bothers me about television," a younger minister remarked. "I don't like the image of TV preachers. However, when I look for an alternative approach to gain mass appeal, I'm at a loss as to what we should do."

"I've heard that before," Ed said. "Our problem is that we lack imagination. Television is a communication tool that we can whittle into any shape we want. A photographer isn't limited to sunsets and weddings. A lot of things can be done with a camera. Even with single-camera productions, you can edit in a variety of sights and sounds. Your problem may be that you are so used to preaching that you can't imagine getting your message across with an interview or a panel discussion or role play or puppets or whatever. The fire-eating preacher has some limited appeal to one segment of the population. Truthfully, television is better suited for eavesdropping—for overhearing an interesting conversation that doesn't have a manifest sales pitch. But most ministers are so cautious on TV that even in a supposedly relaxed interview they look like stained-glass fixtures."

"I like what you're saying," Henry responded, "but how do you act natural with a camera focusing on you?"

"First of all, the camera is not dumping you into a large auditorium with thousands of peering eyes," Ed answered. "Nothing could be further from the truth. Usually, there's just one little person out there taking a break and wondering if you have anything interesting to say. It's like a conversation around a coffee table, with a silent participant disguised as a camera. You talk to the persons in the studio, but you should also acknowledge the existence of this silent ki-

Presentation of self on TV

bitzer looking at you across the room and beyond the walls. You can even smile at this person and make a comment, an aside, in the camera's direction that does not require an answer. Look at the way the professional talk-show host does it. We feel included because the host looks at us occasionally and includes us in the conversation as well as the studio audience. You wouldn't take on a preaching tone with the person or persons you're talking to in the studio. Why do it with the person at home?"

"That sounds good," one minister said, "but we're not used to doing it. What you're suggesting will require some conscious effort. We may look phony at first."

"So you'll improve with practice, right?" Ed smiled. "Television is a land of created illusions, and you'll need some time to get comfortable with it. One thing you may be overlooking on cable access is narrowcasting. Your broadcast doesn't have to have mass appeal. It's legitimate to talk only about your particular denomination. I enjoyed a program given by one of you last week when you discussed the liberal-conservative controversy in your own denomination. It was like eavesdropping. Most denominations have the same problem, so it was interesting."

Another clergyman spoke up. "I'm not sure I would want to talk about anything controversial."

"Then you run the greatest risk of all on television," Ed replied. "You could bore your audience. Television requires new information—or at least something that will challenge our thinking or amuse us or touch a fundamental emotion within us. An intellectual rehashing of something we already know is a turnoff."

"I get tired of hearing TV preachers say they're bringing us something new and exciting," Henry said.

"Because what they actually bring you is something trite and tired out," Ed observed. "It's one thing to promise; it's another to deliver. If what you are presenting really is new and exciting, you don't have to sell it. The content will speak for itself unless you clutter it up with a sloppy or strained presentation."

"Tell us about church advertising on TV," a senior minister of a large church said. "We tried it and didn't like the results."

Church advertising

"In a thirty-second or a one-minute ad," Ed replied, "don't try to give them the whole load of hay. You can't make a significant theological comment in so short a time. Do something people can identify with. The church deals with human drama. A good approach might be to show a brief example of how you care for people and the difference it makes. Let us see you visiting the sick, ministering to the lonely, improving the community, or tending to some other need."

"But how does that make us different from other religious organizations?" the senior minister asked.

"Most people are looking for a church that meets basic needs," Ed replied. "They've seen too many churches that seem interested only in their own survival. What they are looking for is the church that takes its basic mission most seriously. If you can create the perception of a church that cares for people, your ad will be a success. But don't talk about people in the abstract. Show us how you care for a particular group of people—for the elderly, the family, singles, or children. Use a rifle, not a shotgun. Remember, you can't create attitude change on TV. All you can do is make people aware of what you are doing and reinforce what they know they should be doing. Another approach for evangelism might be to target a particular occupational group in the community, such as our hi-tech newcomers, with an ad slanted toward them."

"What can be done with other types of media in advertising?" Henry wanted to know. "What about newspapers and radio?"

"Newspapers are read from left to right," Ed began. "Therefore, you should try for an ad in the upper left-hand corner—if the paper will let you put it there. The best pages are the front and back pages of a section, so-called 'open' pages. Try for a section with a wide readership, such as entertainment or sports. After that, say what you want about your church in as few words as possible. The more words, the less likely it's going to be noticed—too much 'noise' for a casual reader. Also, don't draw a tight border around the ad and fill it up with words. Some blank white space around the words is good for catching attention."

"Give us an example of an effective newspaper ad," one minister suggested.

"Hmm, that's a tough one," Ed answered. "What's effective in one church might not work in another. But as an example of targeting our hi-tech folks, here's a newspaper ad from my own church using a mechanical analogy. It's different, and we had some good phone responses." Ed wrote the ad on the blackboard:

> **Help! Church Needs Replacement Parts**
> New rebuilt members needed for Broadmore Church. Should be self-starting, with fully charged batteries, and able to shift gears automatically. High performance desirable, but an occasional miss understandable. Should be capable of receiving high octane spiritual enrichment, but will tolerate lower-grade input. Open for business at 9 a.m., Sunday mornings, at 1220 Wilshire. Call the Broadmore "service center" at 891-3400 for more information.

"We repeated this ad on radio," Ed continued, "and we're working on a TV production with a woman dressed up as Miss Good Wrench. Some churches may not like this approach, and certainly you don't want to turn off your existing members to gain new ones. Our little church had a lot of fun with it, and no one seemed to object when we showed it to the congregation. You always should test-market your ideas on your congregation before producing them."

"That tells us how to go about it," Henry said. "But are newspaper ads worth doing in the first place?"

"You have to weigh the costs against other media costs," Ed replied, "but newspaper advertising is usually

a good value. You'll reach a small segment of the population that you wouldn't on TV or radio. More important,
you'll build toward a multimedia coverage and reinforce
whatever advertising you're doing already. In fact, if you
use a logo or slogan on TV, you should repeat it in the
newspapers. That expands people's sensory awareness of
who and what you are."

"So what's really needed is a multimedia approach,"
Henry concluded.

"Sure. And don't forget radio," Ed continued. "People
may not be as engrossed in radio as in TV, but a sizable
number of us do listen—especially during drive time when
we're coming home from work. Radio allows us to do
other things while we listen. We don't have to look at a
page or a screen. It's not as obtrusive as TV and, in a way,
it's more suited to the imagination. TV supplies so much
information we don't have to imagine anything. So a one-
minute ad on radio, repeated seven or eight times on a
weekend, is a good investment."

"Why so many repeats?" asked a minister.

"Because radio has a different audience each hour," Ed
answered. "I might also mention that radio stations cater
to distinct groups. If you are trying to target a particular
audience, you'll want to check the survey available at most
stations. Some stations will not reach the people you're
after."

After the seminar, Henry had a chance to visit with Ed
Winters. Ed convinced Henry to try a TV series on the
access channel. Henry was not accustomed to appearing
on television so he was apprehensive, but he felt that Ed
would give him good advice. Two weeks later, Henry
walked bravely into Ed's studio for the opening show of
the series.

"What's the first thing I should do?" Henry asked.

"Put on some makeup," Ed replied.

"Not me, Ed." Henry laughed.

Ed smiled knowingly. "All right, Henry, have a seat on
our little stage. Now let me turn on the five thousand watts

of lighting that you'll need and focus the camera on you. What do you see?"

Henry looked at himself in the monitor.

"I see a blotchy face with sweat on the forehead," Henry acknowledged.

"That's what you look like under TV lighting," Ed said. "Are you really crazy enough to want to do a show like that?"

Henry sighed. "Where's your makeup? I don't want to look like a clown, so give me some help. I've never put on makeup before."

"Nothing to it," Ed said. "Go wash your face and leave it wet. Then take just a little bit of this base makeup, spread it thin, and add a light layer of powder."

"That's all I need to do?" Henry asked.

"Well, a professional newscaster probably wouldn't stop there, but that's enough for us," Ed replied.

"I've got some children coming in to do the show with me," Henry said. "Will they need makeup too?"

"Nope." Ed laughed. "Just us old folks."

Henry put on makeup and was amazed to see how the wrinkles, blotches, and bags under his eyes disappeared.

"Now I feel like a star," he joked. "How do we set up for the show?"

"Let's see." Ed thought for a moment. "You're doing a series on children's sermons. We'll begin with a full shot of you and the kids. Then we'll switch to camera two and shoot over your shoulder. TV is faces, and we want to capture the expressions of the children. Try to get them to talk as much as possible when we focus on them. After that, we'll put the camera on you for a wrap-up."

The show went well for a first in a series, and Ed was pleased. After the children left, Henry stayed around for a cup of coffee.

"This series is exactly the sort of thing we need on the access channel," Ed remarked. "Why can't other ministers come up with programs like this—simple structure, no script needed, appealing faces? There are lots of other great ideas ready to be used. Two entertaining people could talk back and forth doing book reviews, just like movie reviews. Someone could do a series on loving relationships—bring in a psychiatrist. Someone else could do a puppet show. We don't have to be boring!"

"I've heard people talk about media strategies," Henry said. "Is there such a thing?"

"Usually the term 'media strategies' refers to tactics," Ed replied. "For example, you might want to catch people's attention by putting in some movement of the actors rather than just sitting still and facing the camera. Or you might want to put in a visually appealing background with a splash of color, or some snappy underlying music with the introductory titles. Another superb way to catch attention is to come up with a good audience grabber in the first twenty seconds of what you say."

Media tactics

"Such as?"

"Oh, such as 'Have you ever wondered why so many people are depressed at Christmastime?'" Ed tried to think of other examples. "Or try this one: 'If you feel good about yourself, does it mean that you *are* good?' Or 'What good is it to love others as yourself if you wish that you were dead?' I'm sure that you can think of better ones than that, but you get the idea. It's the first twenty seconds that determines whether or not a viewer will want to watch the show—or, for that matter, listen to a radio program or read an article in the newspaper."

"Are there some tactics involved in camera work?"

"Sure, a good example is the subjective angle," Ed answered. "An over-the-shoulder shot focused on the interviewee puts the viewer in the shoes of the interviewer. The viewer gets a sense of being personally answered. In a horror film, a subjective shot lets you become the victim. Certainly a good subjective angle creates greater involvement on the part of the viewer."

"Good camera work could also create a sense of movement," Henry surmised.

"Right—quick cuts, a pan in the right place, or a fast zoom to show action at a dramatic moment," Ed replied. "But the director has to know what's going to happen ahead of time if the shot is going to work. And normally you should use these effects sparingly. If the audience becomes conscious of the camera work, then it's bad work. The camera should not do anything that the human eye would feel uncomfortable in doing. As a viewer, the camera should help me see the scene as I might want to see it."

"I thought that television is a land of illusions," Henry said.

"It is," Ed concurred, "but you have to create the illusions in a way that seems appropriate to the viewer."

"As to overall approaches or strategies for influencing people, do media have any advantages over interpersonal strategies?" Henry asked.

"Not really," Ed replied. "In fact, there are only two strategies open to you with media—role models and making sense."

"In other words," Henry responded, "using someone whom the public can identify with or making sense within their values."

"That's right. Compliance won't work with media in a democratic society," Ed said. "You're left with internalization and identification. The only advantage to media is that you have a wider audience coverage, along with some techniques for gaining attention."

"Television also enhances credibility," Henry noted, "and that's an advantage too."

"Yes, with television that's true," Ed agreed. "But apparently it's less true with radio and newspapers. The more you're on television, the more people think of you as a credible source. You expand your influence as a leader."

Henry continued his series of children's sermons on cable-access television. He found an increasing number of people in the community who recognized him. Also, he was happy to see that the members of his congregation took pride in his programs. Henry could not imagine why other ministers would ignore such a resource.

CONCLUSION

According to research, media set the agenda for attitude change. They do not have the power to bring about change. But nothing is as powerful for creating awareness as the media. In fact, without the media, the diffusion strategy would seem hopeless. Therefore, media can start change but not effect it.

Probably, churches make a mistake if they expect the media to do more than (1) create awareness and (2) reinforce previously held values. The experience of advertising, as well as extensive research in the effects of media, would not promise more than that. Television has the additional advantage of conferring status through regular programming. A leader gains credibility through repeated TV exposures.

Since awareness has great importance as a first step to change, the use of media by churches is vital. Also, the reinforcement effect on one's own members should not be overlooked. We all need visible reminders of the things we like about our church. So in a real sense, the use of media is helpful in building cohesion and community spirit within a congregation.

As already noted, a leader's influence can expand greatly in the community and the church through repeated media appearances—especially television. And a multimedia approach dramatically increases awareness of a basic message when it is simply stated. The more senses that are engaged through a variety of media, the greater the impact. Television, radio, and the print media are tools, not strategies. If the leader knows how to use identification and internalization in interpersonal contexts, then the media offer an extension of those abilities. Henry developed an appealing series of programs with children's sermons. People identify with a church that cares for children and helps them learn. It was a natural extension of the identification strategy.

Henry developed a useful resource through cable access. Television added to his credibility and to the visibility of his church. Henry was already regarded as a leader because he had the basic organizational and interpersonal skills and effectively communicated them within his congregation. The media reinforced that perception of Henry and expanded his leadership role.

8

Summing Up Leadership

After five years of ministry at Highland Church, Henry had a strong sense of confidence in his role as leader. He had a good grasp of the nature of his organization and understood what strategies or approaches were appropriate for particular situations. Since his advice on how things should be managed at the church usually paid off, his credibility had increased with the staff and the board.

One particular change, unnoticed by Henry, took place in his associate, Mary Duncan. Mary had been to a number of seminars on church school education and had watched Henry's pilgrimage as a leader with considerable interest. She had assimilated what she had learned, developing her own leadership style into something of a hybrid. One day she stopped by Henry's office to discuss where she was in her thinking.

"I've come to some new conclusions about myself," Mary began. "It all started when you talked about the difference between me and John Thomas. You called John 'person-oriented' and me 'task-oriented.' I wondered what that meant in terms of my own leadership."

"What did you decide?" Henry asked.

"At first, I thought I might not be suited for church work because the nature of the organization is so closely related to need fulfillment," Mary confessed.

"You felt that a task-oriented person might not fit in?" Henry said.

"Yes. Is that true?" Mary smiled as if she knew the answer to her own question.

"No."

"I don't think so either," Mary continued. "I believe I'm just as concerned for meeting the needs of others as John Thomas. But it took a little while for me to figure that out."

Henry was interested. "Show me how you thought it through."

"Here's a diagram of the strategies for getting things done in the church that I learned from listening to you and the others." Mary gave Henry a familiar chart.

Identification	Internalization	Compliance
Role modeling: works through friendships. People identify with the leader through liking relationships.	Making sense to people: works through shared values. The appeal is through what seems reasonable to the other person.	Rewarding or punishing: works in supervisory situations with consistent monitoring of behavior.

"The strategy that bothered me was identification," Mary said. "It's the main approach for most churches. At first, I couldn't see how a task-oriented person could live with that."

"So?"

"So I learned that the church is filled with as many task-oriented people as person-oriented ones," Mary replied. "In fact, there are so many task-oriented individuals that at least some of our church members will regard me as a friend. I can use the identification strategy as well as anyone else."

"Of course." Henry smiled. "Birds of a feather identify together."

"Also, I discovered that I am not locked into a task-oriented personality," Mary announced. "A part of me enjoys relating to the emotional needs of people."

Henry leaned forward. "I've always suspected that

about you, but I didn't want to insult you by saying it. Very few church workers are a hundred percent task-oriented. We're all service-oriented people and very much concerned about needs."

"Perhaps I was finding it easier to relate to tasks than to people's emotions." Mary was thoughtful. "Remember Sue Lawrence?"

"Yes, she was having problems working through a divorce," Henry responded.

"She came to me for help and I nearly panicked," Mary said. "I've never been married, and I don't know what it's like to go through a divorce."

"What did you say to her?" Henry asked.

"I can't remember," Mary replied. "All I know is that we're fairly good friends now because I listened to her problems. After that, I began to listen to other people's problems."

"You're going to become a regular John Thomas," Henry joked.

"Not a chance." Mary grinned. "I've loosened up a little bit, but I haven't sold out altogether. I'm still seventy-five percent task-oriented. I like sorting things out with written objectives and keeping a chart on the progress of the church school."

"But you've expanded your outlook, and now you are open to versatile management," Henry said.

"I think a person who believes in a locked-in style of leadership is a hopeless case," Mary agreed. "A good leader has to know when to hold and when to fold."

"And when to use compliance and when to use internalization," Henry added.

"It really doesn't help to raise the issue of personality. What matters is your understanding of the organization and appropriate strategies. You can be task-oriented, person-oriented, democratic, authoritarian, or whatever —and it still doesn't indicate what kind of leader you'll be."

"Hmm. You may be underestimating the importance of

personality. But I would agree that the best way to look at leadership is in terms of perceived credibility plus organizational and interpersonal skills."

"I used to think that leadership was only a matter of personality," Mary said. "However, I watched the leaders of my seminars present their subjects. Their personalities differed from one end of the spectrum to the other. But their leadership was tied to how well they communicated interpersonal skills within the organization, not to their personality types."

"Good observation," Henry said. "Many of us get the wrong idea about leadership when we become so enamored of a particular leader that we associate leadership with his or her personality. Then we look at other leaders and try to come up with a composite picture of a leadership personality. We fool ourselves into thinking that leadership is a product of personality."

Mary nodded. "We're better off when we learn to accept our own personality and concentrate on skills. For a while, I felt so defensive about my own task-oriented personality that I couldn't see what was really involved in leadership."

"However"—Henry paused and reflected—"the matching of a particular personality with a given situation may be important. Also, within our culture, some characteristics of personal appearance may be considered as more desirable than others. And then too, as far as personality goes, a charismatic leader might come along—a 'Mozart' with innate abilities."

"So what? The rest of us would still have to *learn* how to play the piano."

"True." Henry laughed. "There's not much point in pondering the charismatic theory of leadership. Even if there are such people, it won't help the rest of us. Most of the leaders that I've known focused on developing their skills. Some also improved their appearance, but their personalities remained the same."

"When we talk about skills, we're referring to both

strategies and tactics," Mary said. "What's the difference between a strategy and a tactic?"

"A strategy is an overall approach or a plan for getting something done," Henry answered. "Tactics are the operations used for putting a plan into action."

"So cognitive dissonance, social judgment, and reward-punishment are tactics," Mary observed.

"And any of these tactics are usable within the three basic strategies: identification, internalization, and compliance," Henry said.

"How do you know which tactic to choose?" Mary asked.

"A basic question that determines the use of a particular tactic is whether you are after a long-range or short-range effect," Henry responded. "A long-range effect ensures a more permanent attitude change and is less obtrusive. Normally, you would use social judgment or a series of reinforcements to accomplish that. But sometimes you'll want an immediate attitude change. Cognitive dissonance works best for a short-range effect, followed by positive and negative reinforcements to make the change more lasting. Dissonance can boomerang if too strong a threat is used. You should use a mild threat with a statement that sounds as if it's for the person's own good."

"Can you use a mixture of tactics and go for a medium-range effect?" Mary wanted to know.

"Sure, you can start with social judgment and add dissonance to speed up the change," Henry answered.

"Isn't this business of strategies and tactics a bit like playing games with people?" Mary queried.

"When you believe that change is important, I don't think it's a *game,*" Henry replied. "Your only choice is an unthinking attempt at change vs. a planned one. For example, I could just start arguing with you and let the chips fall where they may, or I could think about the best way of influencing you without violating your integrity. The latter means I would select a strategy that I think would be ethical. Now, you tell me: Am I playing a game with you?"

Mary laughed. "Well, if you are, it's a more intelligent game than just arguing with me."

"Any time you want to influence a person or persons," Henry said, "you make choices of how you are going to do it. Even Aristotle believed that it is better to make an intelligent assessment of the available means of persuasion than just doing it willy-nilly."

"And the research on behavior regulation gives us our best shot for influencing people," Mary concluded.

"In this century, at least. For the most part, behavior regulation in churches has to be patient and polite. If you are going to try to change me, do it gently and let me feel that I am making my own decision. You can influence me, but don't try to control me."

Mary smiled. "It's nice to feel a sense of participation in changes that affect us."

"Right, even if you influenced me more than I know," Henry acknowledged. "We need each other's influence. The world would be a shallow place without it."

"So we don't have to feel bad about the fact that I want to influence you and you want to influence me," Mary stated.

"Again, the only thing I would feel bad about is an attempt to change me that was insensitive to my feelings." Henry grinned, knowing that such a thing would be difficult to judge.

"And I guess you would forgive me if I erred on that one," Mary said.

"We all step on each other's toes at times," Henry admitted, "especially in churches, where sensitivity is a way of life. Forgiveness needs to be built into us."

"The best changes in churches are the ones that promote healing," Mary said.

"Sometimes, there's a little pain in that healing." Henry remembered his experiences with Harold Robbins and Carol Berger. "But it's worth it."

"Just for the fun of it, what would you say is your favorite strategy?" Mary asked.

Henry reflected. "My favorite strategy is any approach that encourages a sense of growth. The actual strategy could be identification, internalization, or even compliance, in special instances—as long as people have a chance to benefit. I think of tactics the same way."

"I would have thought you'd say identification."

"Since the nature of church organization revolves around need fulfillment, identification would probably be used most often," Henry conceded. "But versatile management is the key. We must stay open to appropriate strategies as new situations arise."

"I guess that with versatile management in churches, you should look carefully at the people involved, try to understand their values, and then think about strategies and tactics," Mary said thoughtfully.

"Yes, you must have a good data base before making a decision as to strategy," Henry replied. "It's important to consult opinion leaders. Without knowing how people feel about a situation, strategies and tactics are meaningless."

"You mentioned at the beginning that credibility is also a must for a leader. How do you build credibility?"

"Credibility has to do with role expectations and how we are perceived as fulfilling them. These expectations differ somewhat depending on the church and the actual position of the minister. For example, as senior minister at Highland, I know that my sermons have to reach a certain level, and my actions during the week must appear trustworthy and reliable. I can't say one thing and then do another—so I have to be careful about what assurances I give. After that, I may gain or lose credibility as I seek to communicate leadership."

"So credibility, or the meeting of basic role expectations, gives you a base on which to build leadership," Mary summarized. "And effective leadership, in turn, will build credibility."

"Yes, if people *perceive* what you do as effective leadership," Henry said. "There's some irony here."

"What do you mean?"

"Well, it's possible that perceived leadership will have no value to God whatsoever," Henry replied. "Leadership in this world means that you have followers who perceive you as a leader. When you read the Bible, you find a lot of leaders who did the opposite of what God wanted."

"Then why not talk about *perceived* leadership and *true* leadership?" Mary tried to answer her own question. "True leadership is doing what God wants, while perceived leadership is doing what people want."

"Not exactly," Henry said. "Perceived leadership may or may not be doing what God wants. True leadership is something on which we make a value judgment through hindsight, and even that may not agree with God's judgment. In fact, our assessment of true leadership is still a perception. We later come to value what someone did, even though that person may not have been regarded as a leader in his or her own time. Some ministers and some historians use the word 'leader' in retrospect as recognition for outstanding service. I don't argue with that—I do it myself. In the pulpit, I would say that two thousand years ago Jesus was perceived as a leader by a few and later proclaimed as a leader by many. Being a perceived leader today means only one thing: that someone has exerted a contemporary influence over many people."

"So the only meaningful way to talk about behavior regulation in the here-and-now is in terms of perceived leadership," Mary said.

"Right. It doesn't mean that the leader is going to heaven, just that the leader has effectively practiced leadership with people." Henry laughed. "It's something we all hope to do within the ethical boundaries of our faith."

CONCLUSION

Only the church offers an environment where emotions and feelings are so intimately linked to one's organizational relationship. The internal sense of "my church" puts a damper on the compliance approach, often used in some business organizations, where behavior is externally motivated through carefully monitored rewards and punishments.

Behavior in churches is more likely to be influenced by such inner-oriented strategies as identification, where the appeal is to friendship, and internalization, where the appeal is to reason within the value structure of others. However, successful leadership in any organization relies on versatile management. Therefore, the third strategy, compliance, cannot be ruled out altogether.

Leadership communicated in the church is a building process; it is a perception that is created and reinforced. The growth of leadership follows a progression:

1. Credibility, the fulfillment of basic role expectations
2. An accurate data base for assessing the values of people within particular situations (opinion leaders should be consulted)
3. An understanding of the nature of church organization
4. Making appropriate use of strategies and tactics for either maintaining a situation or creating change

Most leaders are change agents and risk takers. They like growth and are not content with the status quo. Therefore, a loss of credibility from time to time is typical for a leader, who may step on a few toes in getting from A to B. If a new project is successful, the leader retains credibility. If not, other projects take the place of the one that failed. The point is that leadership means leading people in new productive directions. If the leader becomes paranoid over the possibility of losing credibility, leadership will die of atrophy. There are some needed trade-offs between a possible loss of credibility and getting things done.

A knowledge of strategies and tactics minimizes the risks and makes leadership possible. As long as the leader meets basic role expectations, the congregation will be receptive to leadership communication. A church with leadership that is both effective and ethical is an exciting place to be; it provides each of its members with a role to play in life's greatest drama.